THE AGE

OF

FREE MONEY

ALEKOS VENERIS

Copyright © 2021 by Alekos Veneris

Cover design by Dimitris Angelis

CONTENTS

1. Making money out of thin air   3
2. Money printing as official policy   22
3. The age of free money   96
4. Suggested solutions   115
5. Let's talk about money   133
6. The third pillar   152
7. It is happening   177
8. You are not your work   185

Making money out of thin air

The magic money tree

Is there money tree[1]? Okay, of course, there is no money-making tree. What is meant by the above question? It goes through everyone's mind that the above question is about, whether they can make money without working hard. It is reminiscent of the myth of Midas, who, guided by his greed, asked the god Dionysus for everything he touches to become gold. When Dionysus fulfilled his wish, he quickly realized that he could not touch either his daughter or his food, without turning it into gold. The message of the myth is clear: whoever is too greedy and acquires wealth without effort will commit an insult and will be severely punished. Well, if you think the question of whether there is a money tree concerns all of the above, you are wrong. If you have been misled, it is not your fault, but the politicians, who often refer to the magic money tree. It is usually said that there is no magic money tree, implying or even explicitly stating that, whoever receives an allowance, lives at the expense of those who work. He does all this to win the vote of those who consider themselves to be on the side of the worthy (those who work), pressing on a chronic belief of the people that everything is obtained, after hard work.

But if you think about the question a little better, away from the distorting point of view of political discourse, you will realize that it is much simpler. It could, equivalently, be worded as follows: is there a body that can issue money? The question is now clear, but the answer is not so simple. Speaking of money the first thing one thinks of, is the bank. Suppose someone goes to a bank and gets a loan. It can be housing or consumer loan. Where did this money come from? Did the bank create them out of thin air? One could answer that this money comes from citizens' deposits in the bank. Each bank lends from the deposits made to them. It calculates, how many withdrawals are made and lends the rest of the deposits. It could, for example, have calculated that 15% of the deposits made are enough to cover the daily withdrawals of its customers. The remaining 85% would be available for loans. The interest on the loans would be so much higher than the deposit rate that it would cover the salaries of its employees, its operating expenses and there would be some profit. Is that how things are done? The answer is no.

If you thought that this is how a bank works, it is not your fault again. I also finished a respectable university of economics in Greece and that is what I was taught. It was not considered important to know the origin of money in a university of economics. The aforementioned system was tried, but it did not work because the behavior of the person and therefore of the depositor, can move in a rational framework for most of the time, but in times of insecurity, his rationality and restraint goes away. A rumor or an external event was enough to push a depositor to run to the bank to withdraw his money. The problem was that usually all depositors had the same impulse at the same time. Even if, someone was cool at first, he was eventually forced to go to the bank to demand his money, fearing that those, who had made a withdrawal before him, had run out of bank cash. The so-called bank run was caused. Imagine in the modern age, when all information is spread rapidly and the public sphere is dominated by fake news, how many banking panics would have been caused. Anyone who wanted to damage a country's banking system would simply spread a rumor about a banking problem on social media and a bank run would be inevitable. So things, do not work that way.

In the modern banking system [2], when a bank lends a loan, the amount of money in circulation increases by the same amount. It inflates its balance sheet by entering an asset that is the loan and a liability, which is an equal deposit account of the borrower. The money that the borrower receives is created out of thin air and does not come from the bank deposits. Each bank, of course, is required to have a certain percentage of its deposits, in the form of cash. This percentage is determined by its central bank. In any case, it is not worried about running out of cash, because it can resort to its central bank to give it. All that is needed is for the bank to offer, as collateral, an asset that can be a loan, a bond, etc. For example, it could offer a $ 100,000 loan to the central bank in exchange for $ 100,000 in cash. The money that the central bank gives to the bank under its supervision, is again created out of thin air. The central bank of a country has the absolute right to issue the national currency and can only decide how to use it. In modern times there is no bank run , because the central bank can issue as much money as needed to cover the withdrawals of the citizens of a country. So, those who plan to destroy the banking system withdrawing their deposits at the same time, better think again.

So in the end, contrary to what some politicians claim, there is a money tree ,that is the central bank, without which, the banking system would not be possible to operate. It is no secret. The fact that there is a money tree should be taught in schools and not make an impression on those, who learn it and there should not be people in the public sphere, who claim the opposite. Those who claim, of course, that it does not exist, could reply that the central bank's action is strictly limited to an interbank context.. They would say that the central bank cannot issue money for other reasons beyond this framework. But is that the case? To answer this question we will compare two true stories, concerning financial events. One takes place in the early 18th century and the second in 2008. The second event will then be the starting point of our navigation in the modern financial system.

John Law

The Scotsman John Law[3] operated in France, from 1717 to 1720. During which time, he became chairman of the central bank of France, chairman of the Mississippi company, manager of national dept and tax collector of the state. All this labyrinthine financial edifice in which, he was the ultimate regulator, he named it, with the imaginative name, the System. With his System, he aspired to 'raise France to the highest position that it had ever been found' in his own words. His CV was anything but brilliant, as John Law was a well-known gambler and fugitive for murder, but France's finances were in such a miserable state that his outrageous economic proposals , at the time, were accepted.

The first thing he did was, to establish a royal bank, which had the right to print paper money. It was, in essence, a central bank according to current environment . He later founded the Mississippi Company, which controlled the ¼ of present-day USA. It also issued shares of the company with a starting price of 500 French pounds , which was traded freely, as is the case with shares on today's stock exchanges. All these were new tricks that excited the French, with the result that the demand for shares was huge. He soon issued new shares at a higher price. Why not do it anyway, since he could? In this way his company raised so much money that John Law was able to buy France's public debt and the right to collect its indirect taxes.

The problem that arose was that Louisiana, where his company's exploitation colony was located, turned out to be a suffocating swamp plagued by insects. Within a year, 80% of its settlers had died, either from starvation or from tropical diseases such as yellow fever. Soon the share of the Mississippi company, after the initial rally that led it from 500 French pounds to 10,000, began to fall. At that point, John Law performed a trick that we will see again later. The central bank, which he had founded, guaranteed to buy the shares at a minimum price of 9,000 pounds. For a while, the shareholders were reassured. At the same time, however, inflation was rampant and commodity prices had doubled. The first cracks were beginning to appear in the French confidence in the new banknote and in the shares of the Mississippi company. Both creations of John Law. The fall of the shares, after the temporary pause, continued. Investors gradually stopped believing that a bank issuing paper money that had no intrinsic value, such as coins, could guarantee that the shares of Mississippi Company could retain its value. Law's last move was to reduce the official share price from 9000 French pounds to 5000 and at the same time cut the number of banknotes in circulation in half. He, also, decided to devalue the currency, recalling his earlier promise that this was unlikely to happen. Now every trace of trust in his System had been lost, which collapsed like a paper tower.

The public outcry resulted in the withdrawal of the banknotes, the resumption of the general use of gold and silver coins, and the massive sale of Mississippi's shares. The consequences for France were particularly negative as the Law's bubble and the consequent bankruptcy of the state fatally suspended its economic growth. For many generations the French, after this unpleasant experience, hated paper currency and financial markets. As for John Law, he left France in pursuit and for the rest of his life he gambled in various cities, mainly in Italy, where he died very poor.

The financial crisis of subprime mortgages in 2008[4]

With the description of the second event, we make a big leap in time and are transported to the modern era. Since the 1980s, there have been financial products traded freely on the market, which acted as bonds with collateral mortgage loans (mortgage-backed securities or MBS. When an institution issues a bond it asks for money, which it promises to return to the lender at a specific time in the future, which is the duration of the bond. For example, in a ten-year bond, the borrower promises the lender that he will repay the capital in ten years. Until the bond expires, a fixed or floating interest rate on the capital is paid to the lender at regular intervals. The amount of the coupon that the bond issuer is required to pay depends on how solvent he is considered to be. If it is unlikely that he will not repay the capital he borrowed, he is required to pay a small interest. The opposite happens if it is very possible. From the moment the bond is issued it is traded freely in the market and can change hands. Each new bondholder continues to receive interest / coupon. The price at which the bond is traded depends , again, to a large extent, on the solvency of the borrower. Bond prices fall whenever the bond issuer's financial prospects deteriorate and rise as they improve. Here it should be clarified that the yield of the bonds, which results from dividing their coupon by their price, follows the opposite course from that of their price. This is because while a bond is being traded the price of the bond may fluctuate, but the amount of its coupon remains the same as agreed.

In the modern financial environment, banks can integrate the loans, they have granted, into packages and sell them on the market to obtain additional liquidity. These loan packages are the MBS. They behave like bonds that have as a coupon the installment of the mortgages included in the packages and their price depends on how much prompt payers are those who have taken out these mortgages. When borrowers pay their installments, the corresponding MBS has a high price and low yield. The opposite happens, when a small percentage of borrowers pay their installments.

At the time in the United States, the US government was encouraging banks to lend to the poor with the ultimate goal of reducing inequality. Interest rates were low and everyone rushed to buy a house, with the blessings of the government. The result was that house prices went up sharply. At the same time, the mortgages that were granted became packages and were sold as MBS in the world market. These financial products were considered completely safe. Most traders shunned the fact that their value depends on the ability of vulnerable American households to repay their mortgages.

In 2008, the accumulation of non-performing loans on banks' balance sheets reached its peak. It was realized worldwide that a large part, if not the majority of American households, could not repay their mortgages. Everyone realized that the MBS had no value and hurried to get rid of it. At the same time, however, in the effort to obtain cash, the investors sold out and any other financial product had in their hands. A stock market panic was going on.

The first financial giant to be at risk was Lehman Brothers, which balance sheet was full of MBS. The US financial authorities found themselves in a difficult position. Let the fourth largest US bank collapse or intervene to save it? They had already lowered the key interest rate to almost zero in order to make it easier for banks to lend and for investors to become buyers. Eventually, they preferred to let it go bankrupt, following the dogma of the market. That of creative disaster, which advocates that any company, which cannot survive, is left to go bankrupt, to be replaced by another, more resilient one. All of this, however, is nicely said in sober 'philosophical' discussions on the couch, but is difficult to put into practice. When they let Lehman Brothers go bankrupt, the panic increased and the sell-off expanded and accelerated.. The entire global financial system was in danger of collapsing and some intervention had to be made to save it.

The only way to restore confidence in the system was to find a final buyer of all the MBS, which were on the balance sheets of banks, mutual funds and various investment schemes worldwide.. At the same time, this all-powerful buyer would have to buy also, those companies that were considered systemic, which, if they went bankrupt, such as Lehman Brothers, would endanger the entire financial structure. The collapse of Lehman Brothers was considered a mistake that should not be repeated.

A simple injection of liquidity into these systemic companies would not be enough to save them. A deus ex machina had to be found to save them. Who could it be, when there was no one in the world with so much money? Someone had to be found, who would create them. The only institution that could do this was the US Federal Reserve, which can issue US dollars, which is the world's reserve currency and one that everyone resorts to, when difficult times come. So did the Fed, which created, out of thin air, the dollars it needed to buy all the circulating MBS and US government bonds, that financed the rescue of systemic US companies. The process was the same as we described before, referring to the operation of the banking system .Anyone who wanted to get rid of the mortgage packages would give them to the Fed and it would give them freshly printed dollars in return. As you can see, the central bank turned a blind eye and accepted that the MBS had some value. As for US funding, the Treasury Department issued bonds and gave them to the central bank, which accepted them and exchanged them for hot money.

The problem, that appeared was, that financial institutions outside the United States, which also wanted to get rid of US financial products, did not have access to US dollars, because they could not be issued by their central banks. To save them, too, the Fed consulted with the other central banks and created channels through which it exchanged US dollars with other countries' currencies (swaps). Thus, all the central banks of the world that participated in this exchange process, secured US dollars that they provided to anyone who needed them in their country.

All this did not happen overnight, but in a relatively a short time. The freshly printed US dollars were immediately accepted by all parties and the stability of the financial system was restored. From the following year onwards, the majority of the planet re-entered a trajectory of mild, but steady economic growth. As for inflation, it was never presented.

Conclusions comparing two such distant incidents.

The external environment, in which the above events took place was completely different. The life of a Frenchman in the early 18th century has nothing in common with the life of a modern citizen of a developed country. Most people's homes were slums without running water and electricity, while various diseases were reaping. As for the economic environment, the central bank institution then took its first steps and John Law's 'System' could not be more centralized. The only company that had traded shares, the finance ministry and the central bank were controlled by the same person. In the modern world, the institution of the central bank has been accepted by all and its printing privilege is not disputed by anyone. The parts of the financial system, which are the companies, the banking system and the ministry of finance, are accountable to different people.

There is, however, a basic similarity between the two incidents. In both cases, when things got tough and the investors, in the first case, sold out the shares of the Mississippi company and, in the second, the MBS, the preferred solution was for the central bank to buy what was being sold. This answers the question posed earlier, whether the printing privilege of a central bank is used to guarantee, only, bank deposits and the banking system in general. A comparison of two such different incidents, in terms of the environment in which they occurred, shows that central banks print money in other cases too, if necessary. Central banks have always used their printing privilege in difficult times, something that has not changed, not even today.

The main difference is that in the first case, French investors did not trust their central bank, while in the second, investors around the world trusted the Fed and welcomed the freshly printed US dollars like a manna from heaven. In the first case, John Law's System collapsed, in the second, no. This is interesting. What has mediated the last 300 years that the application of the same recipe has such different results?

At the same time, it seems that the financial crash in France in the early 18th century was limited there, while in the second case, what happened in the US housing market affected the entire planet. It is a sign of how interconnected the world market is, that everything that happens in a small corner of it affects the whole. With that in mind, the US central bank's achievement is becoming even more impressive.

Another fact that one can observe is that in 2008 there was no inflation, even if many trillion new US dollars were created. In the early 18th century, by contrast, the printing of huge quantities of new French pounds led to galloping inflation. What happened in the 18th century may, in fact, seem more logical. When something is produced in large quantities, does it not lose its value? Why then, did the printing of so much money not lead to a loss of their value, that is, to inflation? The answers will be given later.

Finally, it cannot go unnoticed that in 2008 US banks that granted, without adequate risk assessment, housing loans to poor Americans and then packaged and marketed them, were not punished. The same, almost unharmed, came out of the investors who bought the MBS without, too, having made a proper risk assessment . John Law paid for his mistakes, while those involved in the 2008 mortgage crisis continued to be paid well, from various positions in the financial sector, as if nothing, had ever happened. While nowadays, there is a much more sophisticated judicial system, much more transparency in transactions and politicians are theoretically accountable to their constituents, who were directly affected by the 2008 crisis, it was judged that there was no reason to punish those responsible. By no means, does anyone imply that the mob rule of that period , which forced John Law to flee in order to save his life, should prevail today, but the apathetic attitude of authorities continues to raise some questions. At the same time, the rescue of those who had bought risky financial products set a bad precedent. It sent a message to investors that even if they are not careful about what they buy, there is no problem, as the central bank will rescue them anyway. It is paradoxical that the market of the early 18th century was functioning, even if it took its first steps, more justly in relation to today's world market.

Nevertheless, the Fed's intervention was right, even if it rescued banks, companies and investors that was not fair to do. Intervention was needed to restore confidence in the system and prevent the recession from expanding. If the market operated without intervention, many companies worldwide would go bankrupt. It is true that over time some other companies, which would probably be more innovative and resilient, would replace them and the financial system confidence would be gradually restored. The problem is that at this transitional stage many would lose their jobs and poverty would increase. Those who lost their jobs may had to wait another decade for economic activity to show signs of life and find work again. Many, by then, would have stopped looking for work. In our example with John Law, when the, then, new central bank did not have the power to intervene effectively, it took many decades for the French standard of living to improve. The transition period, of course, in modern times would not be so long, but it would be still enough to negatively affect the lives of many people. So, since the Fed and the other central banks of developed countries had the ability to print money, they did well and used it to avoid the worst. But how could they print so much money and be accepted by everyone?

The official version

It all started in the 1990s[5], when central banks became politically independent and implemented policies that curbed inflation. The fact that they became politically independent means that the current state apparatus cannot use them to pursue its own goals. In this way, the central banks gained institutional prestige that makes them credible to all institutions and citizens of each country. Since then, they pursue, the so-called, monetarist policy, while the states pursue fiscal policy, as their revenue and expenditure management is called. At the same time, they adopted modern, at least for the time, economic tools to reduce inflation and to coordinate the banking system and the economic activity of each country. In particular, they have been using, since then, the determination of the short-term interest rate and the targeting of inflation. The interest rate set by the central banks is the interest rate that one bank lends to the other, every day. The reduction of the key interest rate leads to an increase in bank lending and thus to an increase in economic activity. The increase, on the other hand, leads to a decrease in borrowing and consequently to a fall in economic activity. So, when they want to stimulate the economic growth, they reduce the key interest rate, when they want to slow the economic activity, they increase it. As for the targeting of inflation, with its official statements, the central bankers set the bar that inflation will move in the next period, with the result that consumers adjust their behavior accordingly. If the central bank declares that product prices will rise in the near future, consumers will accelerate their purchases before prices rise, thus increasing economic activity. The exact opposite happens when it predicts lower inflation.

So, according to the official version, by 2008 the central banks had won the trust of the people, with the result that their newly printed banknotes were accepted. In addition, with the monetarist policy tools they used, they had reduced inflation. But is that the case? The answer to this question will become apparent to all when we have finished examining the actions of central banks after 2008.

Money printing as official policy

What did the central banks do after 2008?

When the storm passed in 2008 and the situation normalized somewhat, one would expect the emergency measures adopted by the Fed, as well as, the other central banks in the world, to be gradually withdrawn. The central bankers planned to do the same. In particular, the president of the Fed in early 2009, Ben Bernanke, who called the emergency measures taken as 'credit easing' [1], characteristically stated '... because the economy is very weak and inflation is very low. When the economy starts to recover, then it will be time to withdraw these measures, gradually, to raise interest rates, reduce the amount of money in circulation and make sure that we have growth that does not include inflation[2]'.

In essence, he was saying that he planned to follow, literally, the manual followed by the central banks in previous years and was mentioned earlier. According to it, when an economy enters a growth trajectory, central banks raise the key interest rate. As for the reduction in the amount of money in circulation, it meant that the Fed intended to return all US government bonds, MBS and other financial products, which it had accumulated on its balance sheet, to the market. By buying them, they had increased the amount of money in circulation. Selling them, would reduce it. But the precondition set by Ben Bernanke for all this to happen was inflation to rise.

By saying that he wants to achieve 'growth that does not include inflation', he indicates that he expected that the growth of economic activity would lead to an increase in inflation. In 2008, despite the sharp increase in the amount of money in circulation, there was no inflation, but this did not mean that central bankers did not expect it to appear later. It was, therefore, with their hand on the trigger, to withdraw the emergency measures, when inflation appeared. Whenever the general price level rose, it would be a sign that the economy had overheated. An economy in this situation, even if it makes full use of its resources, cannot cope with the increased demand for services and goods, resulting, in an increase in their price. Nevertheless, inflation never appeared.

After 2008, the following ritual was played: the central bankers of the developed countries came out in the press conference and were saying that they set as goal of inflation, to about 2%. Theoretically, consumers and entrepreneurs would get a signal to adjust their behavior. In fact, no one cared about them. Economists, as shown in the first, from the charts below, had repeatedly predicted an increase in inflation, and repeatedly, falling out.

The non-increase in inflation led the central banks of developed countries, contrary to their original plans, to almost never raise their key interest rates. An important exception is the European Central Bank (ECB) in 2011. Through the debt crisis that plagued the European south, including Greece, without a trace of inflation, it rushed raise its key interest rate twice. The result was that the European Union (EU) was in danger of disintegrating. In 2012, acknowledging its mistake, it completely reversed its policy, almost zeroing its key interest rate, without raising it to this day. Of the other central banks in developed countries, only the US Federal Reserve raised it for a short time, from late 2016 to mid-2019, to 2.5% only.

As for the money created by the central banks and channeled into the market, not only did they withdraw it, but they have been steadily increasing it, ever since. As shown in the second diagram below, which shows the balance sheets of the Fed, the ECB and the central bank of Japan from 2008 to 2018, their balance sheets are steadily rising with only a few short breaks. The emergency measures were made permanent. The only thing that changed is that the extraordinary measure of credit easing was renamed as the permanent measure of quantitative easing (QE).

I quote the definition of QE as formulated by the Bank of England itself [3]: 'Quantitative easing is a tool used by central banks, like us, to throw money directly into the economy. Money is either banknotes or digitally like money in your bank account. Quantitative easing includes us who create digital money. Then we use them to buy things like government debt in the form of bonds. You may also hear it as QE or as an asset purchase. It's the same thing. The goal of QE is simple: by creating this' new money 'we aim to boost spending and investment in the economy'. QE has been applied, since then, by all the major central banks in the world, that are these of U.S.A, Europe, Switzerland, Japan, etc. with some small variations between them, in terms of the assets, they buy. In particular, it is implemented by the central banks of developed countries. From 2008 to 2020, the central banks of developing or emerging countries, did not make quantitative easing. Developed countries are those that have strong economies, as opposed to developing ones.

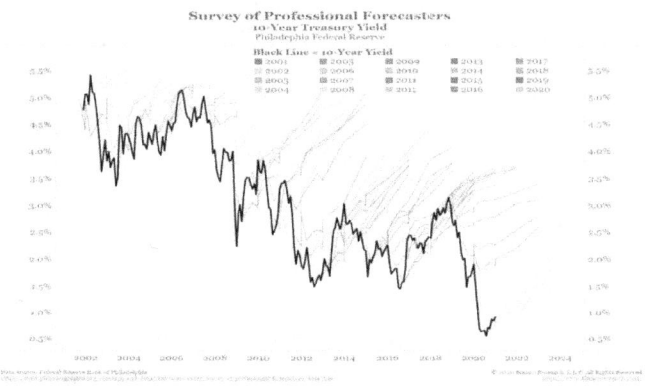

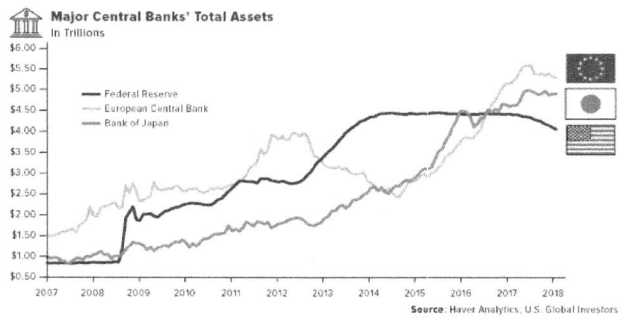

So far, we have learned that the creation of money by central banks is not only used in the context of the operation of the banking system, but also in emergencies. John Law did it in the 18th century, and so did the central bankers in 2008. What changes in the period after 2008 is that money creation out of thin air is announced, for the first time in history, the official policy of central banks, under the name QE. Eventually money tree not only exists, not just is hidden behind the banks, not only appears in crises, but is present from 2008 onwards, affecting the lives of all people with its action. Below we will analyze the consequences of the specific policy of the central banks of developed countries from 2008 until the appearance of the coronavirus, which is another turning point. But before we move on, we will see why all this is done, by the central banks.

The dysfunctional labor channel

The main way, in which money has reached the hands of people, in recent centuries, is through the supply of their labor. Businesses give them money in exchange for working for them. I call the flow of money from companies to employees labor channel. Without it, the whole economic system would collapse, because consumers would not have the money to buy the products and services that companies produce.

Work is the traditional means of achieving social mobility and income transfer. Whoever is not fortunate enough to be the offspring of a wealthy and aristocratic family, the only way he has to rise socially and increase his income is to work hard in his life. Once upon a time things were simpler. Everyone, both graduates and non-graduates, could find a job with a salary, which would be enough to start a family, while, at the same time, their job gave them a prestige in society.

In modern times, things are not so simple. The unskilled find it difficult to find work and when they do find it, they are usually so low paid that their basic expenses are not even covered. At the same time, studying at a university no longer guarantees the graduate's professional future. This is because man is becoming more and more redundant in the production. The following diagram is indicative. It depicts the industrial production of U.S.A, which, although increasing from the 1970s onwards, employs fewer and fewer workers. So when, Trump said he would bring industrial jobs back to US from China, he was lying. And if industrial production returned, the new jobs that would be created, would be much fewer, because, now, industrial production takes place without a significant human presence.

Robots replace humans. This may sound cliché or technophobic, but in this case, it is absolutely true. According to the latest research, each new robot in industrial facilities removes 3.3 jobs[4] from the whole economy. The same picture applies to agriculture and livestock.

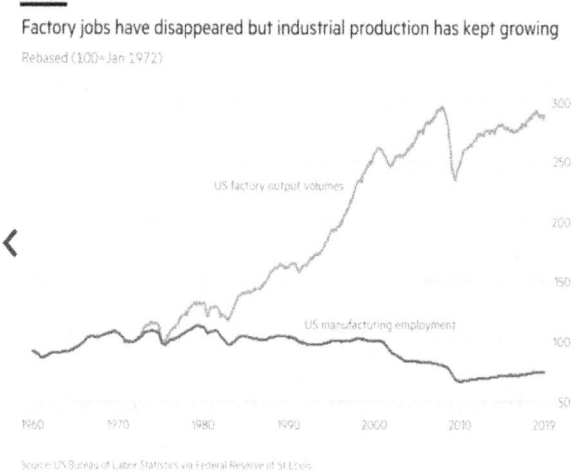

Factory jobs have disappeared but industrial production has kept growing

The permanent optimists accuse those who claim that machines will replace humans in the production process as technophobic. The classic answer is that new professions will be created, which will fill the gap, as was done during the industrial revolution. So, what were those new occupations that replaced the old ones? [5] First of all, new occupations were the operators of machines and production systems, in general, that replaced the manual labor. The above jobs are self-evident that they cannot make up for lost ones. For example, the tractor, with which a field is plowed, needs a driver. But the driver's man-hours to plow a particular piece of land are minimal compared to the man-hours that would have to be devoted to performing the same task in the traditional way. Generally, a machine replaces many workers with very few operators.

The gap has been filled by the so-called tertiary sector or service sector, which provides the majority of jobs in the western world. Now people work not to produce material goods, but to provide services. Specifically, the workforce is absorbed mainly in education, health, retail, legal services, tourism, finance, banking, media, consulting, transportation and catering. The thing is, most of the aforementioned professions have existed for centuries and were created when people started living in cities. Lawyers, secretaries, cooks, accountants, counselors, teachers, entertainers still exist today, as they did in ancient Rome[6]. The migration of more and more people to the cities has led to the multiplication of jobs in the tertiary sector. Few new professions have emerged, and those that have emerged employ very few. One could, therefore, say that the widespread narrative that new professions are gradually replacing the old ones is just a myth, which has little to do with reality.

Focusing our attention, now, on the tertiary sector, which mainly maintains current employment at relatively high levels, one cannot help but notice that, it was and remains particularly vulnerable to changes in external conditions. A major weakness is that its survival depends on the general state of the economy. In order to consume services, one must have some income and be in a good mood, which are not self-evident in times of crisis. Thus, in any recession of an economy, the sector most affected is the tertiary. In addition, in order to survive, it requires a critical mass of above-average income consumers. If it were not for those consumers who can and do spend a little more, the firms that provide services would not survive. At this point, at least, the system helps.

In recent decades, many administrative jobs have been created, covering a part of the lost jobs, both in the public and in the private sector. Even large private companies have, on average, 7 levels of management hierarchy. It is the so-called bureaucracy. Bureaucratic jobs, often, do not make financial sense for the organization that creates them. The extra revenue they offer is often less than the extra expense they incur. In addition, they are a way of perpetuating inequality. Usually, these positions are occupied by rich children whose parents have the money to send them to universities, with very high tuition fees. Who, after all, to occupy administrative positions, if not the rich kids? Apart from the negatives, however, bureaucratic jobs are the oxygen of the tertiary sector, because they are usually well-paid jobs and their owners ask for various expensive services. Their existence, also maintains financial, many private universities that offer various expensive postgraduate programs in business administration (MBA). The great dependence of most companies that offer services, on the situation of their richest customers, is an additional disadvantage.

The problems of the tertiary sector do not stop here. In recent years, technological developments have not left it unaffected. The planet's interconnection via the internet at ever-increasing speeds and the rapid growth of computing power have radically changed the environment in many industries. Many services are now performed without the need for human presence. For example, international trading platforms are increasingly making banks' physical branches redundant. At the same time, the tremendous progress made in recent years in artificial intelligence threatens to shrink entire sectors such as transport, consulting firms, law firms, media, etc.

Finally, most companies offering services are usually small and medium-sized, competing with large multinationals. The only way they can do this is by reducing their costs. Often only labor costs can be reduced. So most people employed in the service sector receive low wages.

Labor channel malfunction is a chronic problem that is not easily solved. Somewhere here, the central banks are coming to offer the solution which, as they claim, is to increase investments. As you recall in the definition of QE by the Bank of England, it stated that its goal is to increase investment and consumption. In essence, he says, increasing investment will lead to new jobs, which will increase the world's disposable income and ultimately consumption. The agencies that can make investments are, mainly, the big companies and the states and that is why the central banks make sure that they have plenty of money at their disposal. In addition, the state can make social expenditures, giving unemployment benefits to those who do not work, and supplementing the income of low-wage and other vulnerable groups. In essence, central banks support the two pillars of the system, which are the multinationals and the states. The two pillars, in theory, know better how to manage money to save the labor channel and the people. We will see later if they have achieved this after 2008.

The consequences of QE

QE and financial markets

The Bank of England, in the definition of QE, stated that it buys assets. What are these? They mean financial products that are traded on the world market and liquidated at any time. The big central banks of the western world, which are those of the USA, the EU, Japan and Switzerland, since 2008 with some small fluctuations, buy mainly government bonds. The Fed did not buy corporate bonds until the advent of Covid-19. The rest were buying. The central bank of Japan, which first adopted the QE, even buys stocks. The MBS, which caused the crisis of 2008, continues to be accumulated by the central banks. But, why do they do that? Why do they buy government bonds with the money they create? The answer is to support the market, which raises a new question: why support the market?

The institution, which has always been considered the most suitable for the distribution of capital in the western world, is the market. The market rewards innovative and productive companies by lending them at low interest rates. It does the same in countries with good fiscal indicators. At the same time, it punishes unprofitable companies and states with high deficits by not financing them at all or financing them at very high interest rates. According to the financial manuals, the market ensures the financial discipline of states and companies and that is why it was chosen that through it the money of the central banks will flow. So the central banks support the market and somewhere here the contradictions begin, which are integrated in QE.

You see, it is contradictory the central banks to use the market as a vehicle to distribute the money in a fair way and at the same time to support it. When they support it, it means , with their interventions, they distort its function. It ceases to operate in a fair and impartial manner and its discipline is not imposed on states and companies. When central banks buy, for example, a country's government bonds, they reduce the country's borrowing market rate. In practice, then, central banks use only the market network to distribute the money they print and to signal to private investors that everything is fine. So the immediate consequence of QE may not be the support of employment, but it is certainly the continuous rise of markets.

The continuous rise of markets.

Since the adoption of QE as the core policy of central banks, the behavior of financial markets has completely transformed, with all that entails. The chart below shows the combined value of stocks and bonds worldwide, from 2008 to 2019. It seems that their value is constantly rising, which is due to the action of central banks. One could, of course, say that this is happening simply, because the global economy is constantly growing and QE has nothing to do with it. He would, however, have some difficulty explaining how, while global GDP from 2008 to 2019 has increased by, about, 50%, at the same time, WORLD.MSCI which is the global stock value index, has almost tripled and the American S&P has more than quadrupled.

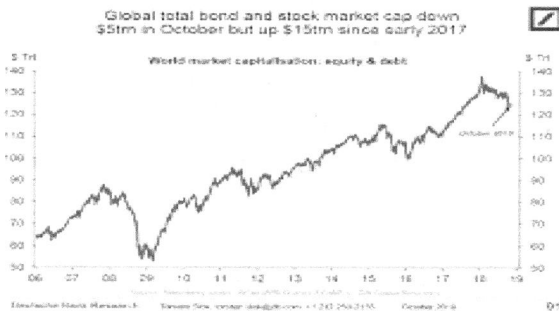

The central banks are co-responsible, because they appear as the ultimate buyers of all the financial products that circulate in the world market. It must be understood that the markets do not go up because the central banks buy all the shares and all the bonds. It happens because they guarantee that, if necessary, they will buy anything that private investors are not willing to buy. Usually, buying a central bank with created money, only government bonds, which are the foundation of financial markets, supports the whole edifice. For example, the Fed, in the period shown in the chart above, did not buy stocks , which means that they did not rise, because it bought them . They went up because the Fed has signaled that they will not let US markets fall for any reason. So reassured investors bought US stocks as well. The same guarantee was given by the other central banks, raising the value of all financial products worldwide.

The commitment made by central bankers is informal. There is no law that dictates that they intervene in the markets The only way to prove their commitment is in practice, whenever necessary. So they do. This happened, for example, in October 2019, a few months before the coronavirus appeared. By October 2019, the Fed had raised its key interest rate to 2.5% and was timidly trying to withdraw the money it had created. This can be seen in a previous chart showing the balance sheets of central banks. In other words, it was trying to return to the traditional exercise of monetarist policy, which FED knew in previous decades. At that time, the cash of American banks was found to be insufficient to purchase all the bonds issued by the US Treasury Department. The interbank interest rate soared in one day. At the same time, there were not many willing buyers from other countries to buy American bonds, because the dollar was very expensive then. Simply put, the USA had such high financing needs that no one could lend to them, even if it is the largest economy in the world. If you do not remember any crash, it is because it did not happen. This malfunction was only reflected in the increase of an interbank rate (repo rate). The end result was the Fed to abandon the plan ,to return to normalcy immediately and start buying government bonds with new money, increasing its balance sheet again. And all this happened, even before the appearance of Covid-19. The Fed had demonstrated once again that it would intervene whenever necessary. It did not happen during the same period, not even some stock market turmoil. Happy investors were buying stocks, bonds, etc., knowing that the central banks were covering their backs.[7]

The support that central banks offer to the markets affects, without exaggeration, the lives of all people. From the first steps of capitalism until 2008, the global financial market affected all the countries of the world. But, from 2008 onwards, there was a surge in its gravity across the spectrum of human activities. The world market is like a cloud that has covered the whole planet and is constantly expanding. No one can ignore it and that is why the consequences of QE are more easily understood by examining the behavior of market participants, which will happen later.

The finance market players

Bankers that do not give loans.

On paper, QE is applied to finance banks and these in turn businesses. Because of their traditional role as money brokers, banks are often referred to as the heart of the financial system. Even today, many are trying to convince people that QE is nothing more than an interbank transaction. The reality is completely different.

As soon as 2008 passed and the system was saved at the last minute, many suggested that banks should return to traditional banking, which is to accept deposits and give loans, which they will not make after packages, in order to sell them. Their investment activities would be completely separated from the purely banking part[8]. The previous policy proposals were correct. Banks have no business engaging in financial activities. Creating and distributing financial products, in which often no proper risk assessment can be made, contributes to the instability of the system. Just as it did in 2008.

In retrospect, those who argued the obvious seem naive . Not only did the banks move away from their investment activities, but they inflated them so much that they also outperformed the banking ones. As mentioned earlier, a strategic choice was made to distribute the money through the market (capital market-based model) and not, consequently, through the banks (bank-based model) [9]. Under normal circumstances, direct financing of companies and the state through the market is preferable and fairer, than done through intermediaries banks. With QE, however, the market, as mentioned, is completely distorted, so the arguments against the bank-based model disappear. The real reasons why the market has established itself as the almost exclusive intermediary of money, unfortunately, are unknown. There can only be suspicions that the financial sector was so strong that it did not allow it to lose its importance.

In an environment dominated by financing through bonds and not through banks, the latter have no reason to exist. This does not mean that central banks did not endow them with liquidity to lend. Banks had infinite liquidity. They just did not have the motivation to give a lot of loans. The European banks and especially those of the European south, after 2008 found themselves with loans, many, if not most of which, were in arrears or uncollectible. As a result, most European banks were reluctant to give out new loans for fear of becoming uncollectible as well and further burdening their balance sheets[10].

However, one would expect banks with strong balance sheets, like the American ones, to lend without hesitation, since they had such cheap and uninterrupted financing. Unfortunately, even in this case, the granting of loans was not as expected. Bankers were especially wary of lending and were asking for more collaterals after 2008. They did not want to be stigmatized, again, for taking advantage of the poor by lending, as was the case with mortgages before 2008. When, in addition, they had ways to make easier profits, they preferred them. They chose to ride the wave of markets that their bosses induced.

The easy profits, in recent years, come from their involvement with the markets. In other words, instead of lenders of the capital, they became its managers. Taking a look at the balance sheet of Morgan Stanley, which is the largest bank in the western world, one finds that, in recent years, the interest income from loans has been about a meager 10% of their total income[11] About half of their revenue comes from managing their wealthy clients' portfolios. (In any case, the central banks are making sure that the markets go up. What could be easier than investing the money of their wealthy friends receiving a high commission ?) Another main source of income is the commissions they charge for their mediation in bond issuance. (Many bond issues with the blessings of central banks mean a lot of easy bank profits.) One last source of revenue is the profits from trading in financial products, which they conduct for themselves. (Having infinite liquidity as opposed to private investors, it is much easier for them to make high profits.)

Bankers may enjoy great prestige and be paid a lot of money, but their role is , nowadays, decorative. Not to mention the online banking applications (fintech), which are gradually replacing them. Their profits now come mainly from commissions on the growing transactions of financial products. It should also be mentioned another function performed by the banks, which, without changing the final result, is important for how the system looks from the outside. As has been said, at every opportunity the central banks declare their political independence, while, at the same time, they buy government bonds. But if that were the case, one could accuse them of buying government bonds directly, financing the state directly and therefore not being politically independent. In fact, this is exactly what is happening, but the central banks get offended, if their political independence is challenged. So, in order to seem legal, they instruct the banks to buy the government bonds first and then buy the bonds from them in the so-called secondary market[12]. So the central banks continue to declare that they are independent agencies, without being too ashamed.

Investment funds

But beyond the bankers, there are the classic fund managers, whose work has been made easier and more profitable, by the central banks. It has become easier, because the markets are just going up. For example, the average annual return of the main US S&P index over the last ten years is 13.6%. It has become more lucrative because they are paid commissions on the capital they manage. Thus, as the volume and value of financial transactions increase, so do their commissions. It is estimated that investors pay 1.3% of their total investment to their fund managers each year, which in thirty years, translates into 1/3 of the initial investment. While, whoever wants specialized financial services (hedge funds, private equity funds, venture capital funds) is charged every year from 3% to 5% on his capital[13]. The exorbitant fees charged by fund managers should not impress. It is logical that as the funds increase in volume, so does the importance of their managers . Since profits create the desire for new profits, it is normal, those who promise to achieve them to, be paid generously.

The bubble of vanity

Venture capitals[14] invest in start-ups, which are mainly active in the field of technology, in exchange for a percentage of their share capital. Their goal is to expand the start-ups so that they can be listed on the stock exchange and venture capitals can redeem their shares, earning high profits. The value of the funding provided by venture capitals, as shown in the chart below, has skyrocketed since 2009.

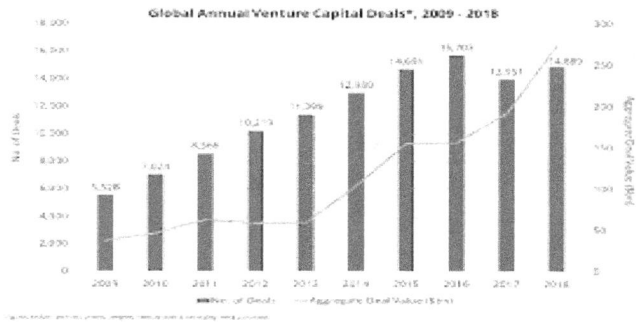

This is not accidental. It is, again, indicative of the distortions created by central banks in the markets. By supporting them in every way, they protect the capital that circulates in the market. Its protection then leads to its multiplication and a constant search for new channels. Venture capitals are an attractive destination for capital, because in addition to the promise of high profits they provide, the participants are highly recognized. The start-ups, in which they invest, aspire to become the next big technology companies that will change the world. Each aspires to become the next Apple, Google, Amazon, etc. The start-ups that exceed capitalization of 1 billion and have not been listed on the stock market, are called unicorns, which are mythical creatures. Naming them like this emphasizes their uniqueness . Already, the vanity that prevails there, is becoming apparent.

The reality is completely different, again. Few of these technology companies have managed to emerge from obscurity. They have not created something truly innovative, despite the lot of buzz. The chart below shows the accumulated financial results of the most successful venture capital investments. All these 'unicorns' from 2014 to 2018 have losses. Do not think that this has changed nowadays.

An immediate question that arises is how venture capitals make profits. One way is for investors to sell their stake to others, more expensively, which is possible because there are many rounds of financing in start-ups and there is generally a lot of opacity in trading. One reason they are not listed on the stock exchange, which would force them to disclose their financial data, is to maintain the opacity regime that prevails in their financing. In general, the industry is plagued, in addition to vanity, by corruption and frequent scandals. Beyond that, venture capitalists who hold their positions, instead of pursuing a prudent economic policy, usually put even more money into start-ups , which seems somewhat contradictory, if they were aiming for profit. Everything will become more understandable when, we see how they work.

The basic model of operation and development of 'unicorns' is, first, to create a digital platform / application and then to do aggressive marketing. Through smartphones, which more and more people around the world have, they offer their services. Through social media, they are advertised and use the cloud for expansion, whenever needed. That is, they use an online infrastructure that already exists, and all they create, is a smartphone application. At the same time, they offer their services below cost in order to gain a larger clientele. Their master plan is that, when they get a lot of users, they will increase the subscriptions they charge and become profitable. By 2020, almost no unicorn company had achieved this.

The trick, so that venture capitals do not suffer losses, is the, technically, high valuation of start-ups and therefore their shares. Various analysts make high estimates in the valuation of start-ups, always referring, to the high prospects they have. Theoretically they have high prospects, because they can make customers, through the internet, all of humanity. To achieve this they must have recognition, which is achieved through aggressive marketing. So their wealthy investors spend huge sums of money for ads and promotions to make them world famous. In this way, two things are achieved at the same time: a) The large amount of money that rich investors have and do not know what to do, finds a way out and b) on paper, at least, the value of their holdings goes up.

Expanding clientele of start-ups, may not even cover advertising costs, but this is not a problem for investment funds. The flow of capital to loss-making companies has been going on for over a decade. The bubble is just growing. Most venture capitalists, at least until 2020, were reluctant to list their technology companies (IPO). Even if the market, after 2008, is supported by the central banks, their investment bubble is so large that they were not willing to risk it. From all this process, of course, comes something positive that must be mentioned. Often these 'unicorns' offer services very cheaply, benefiting consumers. There are, for example, delivery companies, which charge for what someone orders cheaper, than what the customer would be charged if he bought it himself from the order store.

Finally, the wealthy investors of venture capitals are not so much interested in the product or service that their start-up company will offer. They are mainly interested in, what it offers, to be accompanied by an attractive message and well-designed graphics, which will allow them to run an expensive advertising campaign, where they will channel their money. If this message, moreover, flatters them, even better. As soon as, they ask for it, this is, what the aspiring young entrepreneurs, offer them. After all, it is easier for ambitious young people, than to discover something new and come up with a detailed business plan, to make a nice slogan. So while all the "unicorns" promise to change the world, talk about authentic experiences, activism, love and the like, all they actually offer is another mobile app.

None of this could have happened if the central banks had not intervened in the market. Such high valuations of start-up technology companies are possible, because everyone knows that no matter what happens, the central banks will intervene, not letting the bubbles burst. It allows companies that have been unprofitable for more than a decade and have nothing to offer, not only to survive, but also to be projected, as those who open new avenues for humanity.

The players who issue bonds

The most favored of these conditions, created by central banks in the markets, are the participants who issue bonds. Fund managers cannot directly access the capital, they manage. They can only charge commissions to it. But those, which can issue bonds , gain direct access to capital, with the blessings of the entire financial system. These bodies are the two pillars of the system: the states and the big companies. Their borrowing costs have been steadily declining, since 2008.

Any institution that issues bonds increases its debt accordingly. Debt, however, is gradually becoming less taboo. After all, what is the debt, from a simple number, which in this case, just grows? Corporate debt, gradually, is reported less and less. Many, large and well-known companies have high debt that no person in the public sphere or investor cares about. Regarding government debt, the debt-to-gross domestic product (GDP) ratio is reported more frequently. Gradually the debt tolerance becomes greater. Once 60% debt / GDP was considered a milestone. Any country that owed debt above this milestone was considered to have a problem. Since 2008, the milestones have been gradually increasing. Below we will see, how they used the much money that the companies and the states had at their disposal.

Companies that issue bonds

From the moment, the big companies had the option to borrow cheaply and as much, as they wanted, so they did. The chart on the left shows the increase in corporate bonds issuance, while the one on the right shows the rapid decline in borrowing costs since 2008. The great advantage of bond issuers over small and medium-sized companies, which are forced to rely on banks to gain liquidity, is being realized. Since 2008, the gap between large and small companies has widened. Small and medium-sized businesses are forced to compete with large ones that are connected, through markets, to the source of money.

Corporate Bond Issuance Is Increasingly in the Lower End of Investment Grade

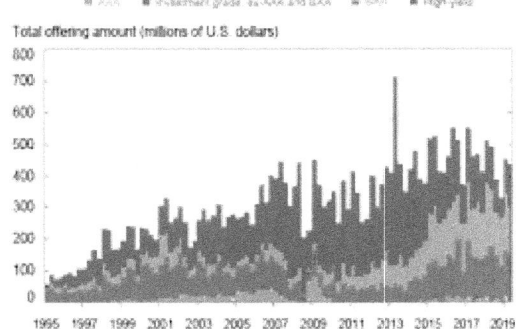

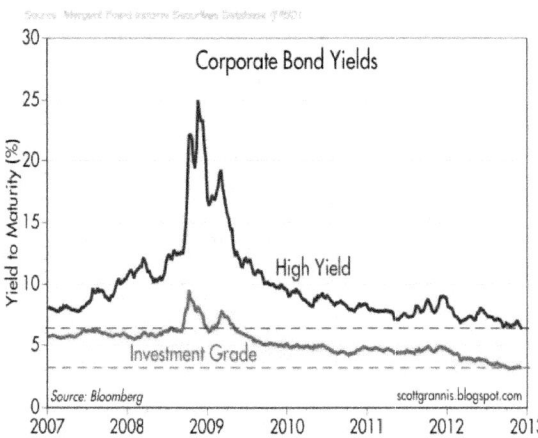

Where did the companies' money go?

Dividend's increase[15]

Let's try to get into the position of a CEO of a large company, which has plenty of cash. It makes sense that after giving a large salary to himself, he would take care to satisfy his shareholders, in order not to lose his position. The shareholders of a company, like all the people of the world, feel better, if they have more money in their pocket. A shareholder's pocket swells, if he receives large dividends. Indeed, as shown in the chart below, US corporate dividends on net profits have been steadily rising, since they plunged in 2008. The same trend is observed worldwide. In addition, they have found a new method to reward their shareholders. They buy own shares, which they then abolish. Thus the shareholder enjoys a higher dividend yield. It seems, somewhat unthinkable, to spend money like this. They are essentially burning money. But it is now considered a common practice, especially for American companies.

Deals instead of investments

Another way for big companies to spend their money is to acquire another company or merge with it. As can be seen from the chart below, the volume of mergers and acquisitions has been growing steadily, since 2008. Corporate agreements have always been easier than investing in research and development. Additionally, everyone likes deals. Shareholders are excited about the prospect of potential high future profits. The financial press acquires material to publish, with possible scenarios, intrigues, etc. State regulators often intervene, reminding everyone who has the power. The more deals are made, the more commissions the intermediaries, ie the bankers, earn. Another reason that very large companies like acquisitions is because they can acquire smaller companies before they become competitors. In 2020, US and EU competition regulators, after years of inaction, blame Silicon Valley giants such as Facebook and Google for just that.

Zombie companies

However, not all companies are big, that acquire the others. There are, also the firms that just survive , taking advantage of the favorable conditions in the bond market. These are called zombies. Their main feature is that their profits (if any) are not enough to cover the interest on their loans. The chart below shows the increase in the number of zombie companies trading on various stock exchanges around the world, from 2008 to 2018. The zombie companies, with each new bond they issue, repay the interest and capital of the older issues. Many small and medium-sized enterprises are also zombies, which banks continue to lend to them, because otherwise they would be forced to record their previous outstanding loans as losses, on their balance sheets. They lend more easily to bankrupt old companies than to new ones.

The increase in the number of zombie companies is a negative situation. Not only that, they do not invest in research. What's worse is, that zombie companies prevent others from entering the industry, in which they operate, because they are gaining a significant market share, which would be necessary for the profitability of a new company. Thus, often, an industry can only consist of loss-making companies, in which their employees are underpaid and do not even have the opportunity to find a better paid job in their field, unless, they emigrate[16].

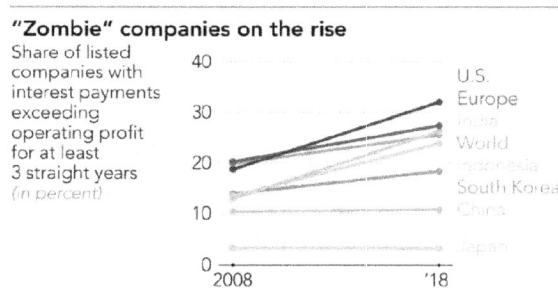

Source: Nikkei (2019)

**FIGURE 1
ZOMBIE COMPANIES ON THE RISE**

Increased investment in research and development

The money of the companies were not only wasted, in high dividends, purchases of own shares and deals. Part of them, was dedicated to research and development, which is a positive development. This success can be credited, to some extent, to the financial conditions the central banks created. It is clear from the chart below, that the amounts invested in research and development after 2008, especially in the US, China and the EU, showed a significant increase. China is a special case, which, we will discuss later. China's central bank , however, pursued an expansionary credit policy, as have the other major central banks in the world. A company's research and development investments are aimed at either improving existing products and services or creating new ones. When a new product or service is created, the whole society benefits, because new businesses are created, which means new jobs.

Gross domestic expenditures on R&D, by selected region, country, or economy: 2000–15

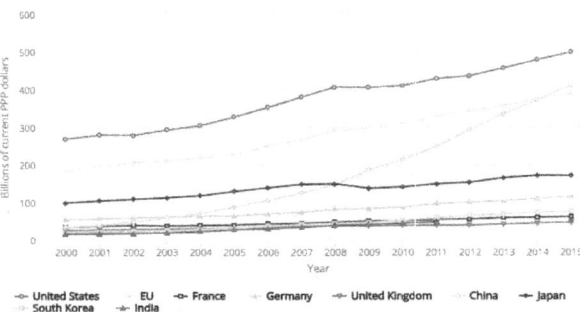

EU = European Union; PPP = purchasing power parity.

Note(s)

Data are for the top eight R&D-performing countries and the entire EU. Data are not available for all countries for all years. Data for the United States in this figure reflect international standards for calculating gross expenditures on R&D, which vary slightly from the National Science Foundation's protocol for tallying U.S. total R&D.

The powerful state

In the end, we left the biggest player in the market, which is the state. Government bonds, and especially those of the United States, are considered the basis of the entire financial structure. The first concern of central banks was and is to support the public sector. QE mainly consists of the purchase of government bonds. The fact that they declare themselves independent from the public sector means nothing anymore. The main reason central banks became independent in the 1990s was to prevent the public sector from squandering fresh printed money. Then, when this was happening, the money was losing its value and inflation was created. After 2008, everything has changed. Central bankers have found that when they print money, inflation does not come. Since 2008, instead of the central bankers preventing the state from using new money for spending, they have been asking it to do so. This is the main argument of various eminent economists. They say that the central banks did what they could in the framework of their monetarist policy and that the public sector has to respond with fiscal interventions. This means, in simple terms, that the central banks have printed plenty of money and the states must use it, increasing their spending.

By intervening on a regular basis in the government bond market, central banks have reduced the cost of government borrowing to very low levels. Borrowing costs have fallen even for countries, which central banks have not made QE. The support of the bond market by the central banks of developed economies was enough to lower lending rates in emerging economies as well. This is clearly seen in the first, from the two diagrams below. The average interest rate in the ten-year bond of developed economies, as it seems, was falling steadily, so that in 2017, it was below 2%. The corresponding average lending rate of emerging economies in 2017 fell to 6%. The downward trend in lending rates of states continued in the following years. States took advantage of their low borrowing costs and increased their debt. As can be seen, in the second of the following charts, after a stabilization of global debt at the beginning of the first decade of the 21st century, since 2008, it has been growing steadily. Below we will see how they used the money that the states had at their disposal.

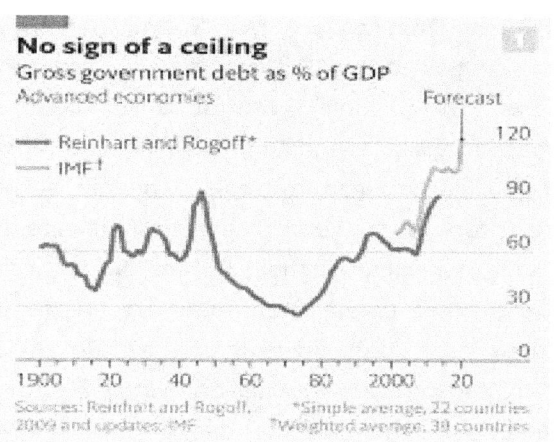

How did the states spend the money?

The following charts show the trends that prevailed after 2008 in terms of public spending. As has been said, central banks make sure that states have the money to supplement their citizens' incomes with social benefits and to make public investments. The first diagram shows that public sector social benefits in countries, that are a representative sample of the western world, either increased slightly or remained stable. These benefits are for the unemployed, disabled and poor families, as well as funds for health, education and training programs for the workforce. One can see that social spending has been rising since the 1960s anyway, so this trend is not due to the action of central banks. The gradual increase in social spending arose from the moment that machines began to replace people at work. States intervened to compensate, to some extent, for the loss of income of their citizens. So the central banks did not create the trend, but helped it to continue after 2008, even if only a little. What is striking and contrary to what one would expect and reflected in the second diagram is that the investments of the developed western countries in infrastructure decreased after 2008. While their central banks provided them with ample financing, they chose to do not use it to increase their public investment.

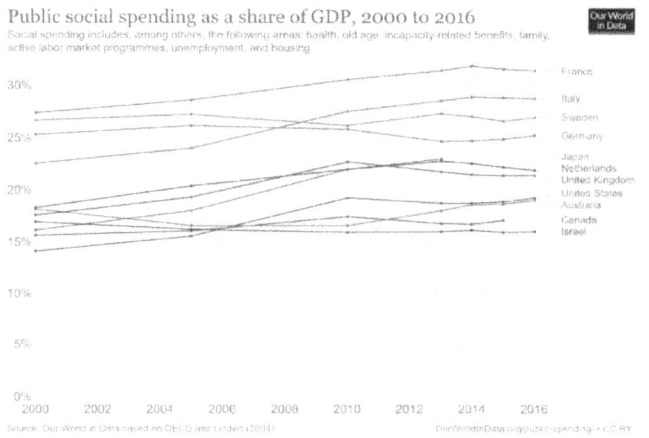

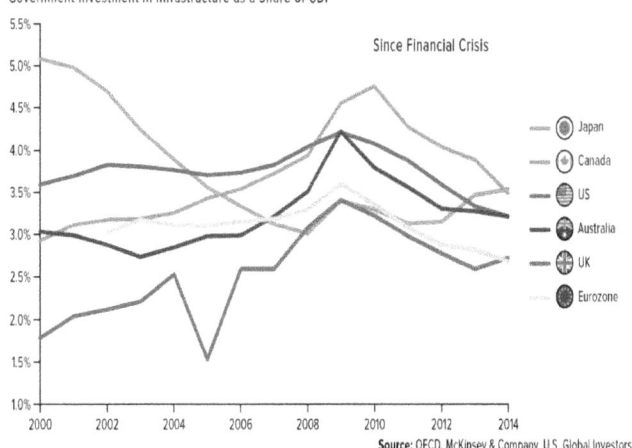

Mixed results

Increasing inequality

After what has been said before, it makes sense that inequality has increased. The main mechanism for inflating inequalities was the market. The chart below shows who owns the stocks of US market, which is the largest in the world, depending on the income scale to which they belong, from 1990 to the first quarter of 2020. It seems that the richest 1% is gradually increasing its share , until the beginning of 2020 they held more than half of the traded shares. At the same time, those who belonged to the 10% of the richest people owned 87% of the shares, while half of the population owned almost none.

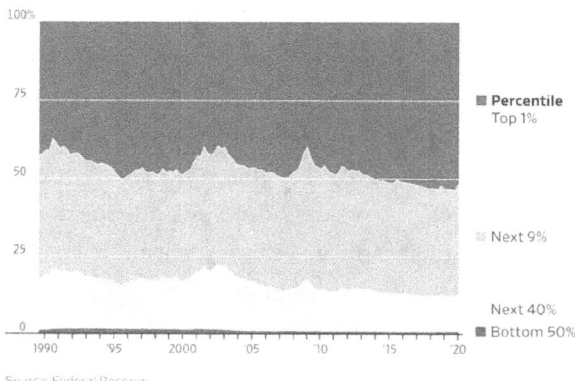

Shares of Wealth
The top 10% of earners owned 87% of all U.S. stocks outstanding in the first quarter of 2020.

Source: Federal Reserve

Central banks, by supporting market indices, make the rich richer. The rich, as one would expect, anyway, own almost the majority of financial products and when their value increases they become richer. At the same time they receive dividends from shares and coupons from bonds. The process of enrichment does not stop here. Every time the market rises and the rich get richer, the foundations are laid for a new rise of the markets and therefore of their wealth. The reason is that the already rich have no place to channel their extra income. How many extra cars, houses and, in general, consumer goods to buy? There is saturation at personal consumption from one point onwards. The end result is that the rich channel the extra income back into the markets, inflating them even further.[17]

Goal of the central banks was with their actions to increase consumption, which would lead to an increase in business profits, which would lead to an increase in recruitment by companies to meet the increased demand, which would lead to an increase in available income, which would again lead to a new increase in consumption. They wanted to achieve this virtuous cycle, but, unfortunately, the cycle they seem to have achieved, surely, was the initial rise of the markets to lead to a new rise and to make the rich richer.

After all, it does not surprise us that the income of those who belong to the 1% of the richest people continues to grow, as shown in the chart below. Rising inequality began in the 1980s. In 1965, the CEO of a top 350 U.S. company was paid about 20 times more than the average employee. In 1980, he received a salary about 30 times higher. In 2015, the CEOs of the largest companies in the United States were paid, approximately, 300 times more money, than an average employee. [18]

The inequality, again, was not caused by the central banks, but it is they, who not only maintain it, but expand it to unimaginable levels. Inequality emerged in the 1980s, when large multinational corporations gradually began to use new technologies in the production. At the same time, they could sell their products, due to the deepening of globalization, all over the world. The result was that multinationals increased their sales and, at the same time, reduced their costs.. Their high profits led to an increase in their market value and an increase in the salaries of their executives. Inequality had emerged. Those who held a good position in a multinational were paid disproportionately more than all other employees. The main shareholders of large companies were equally benefited. It was an unfair situation, but at least, the extra income enjoyed by a small portion of people was based on real profits made by multinational corporations. After 2008, their high valuations and high liquidity, which is used by their executives to give huge salaries to themselves, is due, in large part, to the money printed by central banks.. And while a company's profits have a ceiling, defined by its sales, the money that central banks can print has no ceiling. The modern rich are literally connected to an inexhaustible source of money, which is very dangerous.

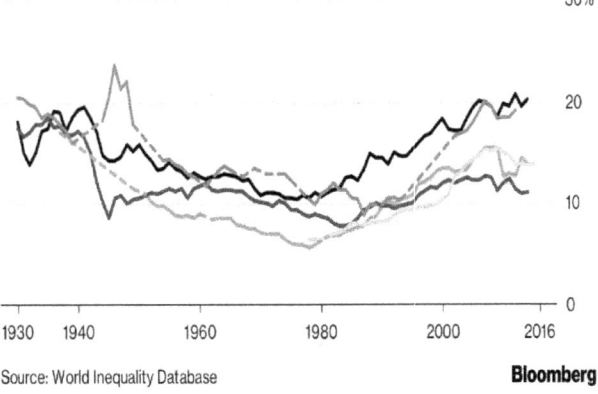

The Return of the Rich
Income share of the top 1 percent of earners
/ U.S. / U.K. / France   China / South Africa

Source: World Inequality Database — Bloomberg

Reduction of unemployment but..

So far, money printing seems to have had a negative effect. If we stopped at this point and the central bankers read what has been written, they would protest saying that it was not mentioned that they dropped unemployment. They would be right. As the diagrams below show, unemployment among the general population and young people, in particular, in a representative set of countries around the world, has been steadily declining since 2008. The only major exceptions were Greece, Spain and Italy, which due to the debt crisis in 2011, were slow to follow the general trend.

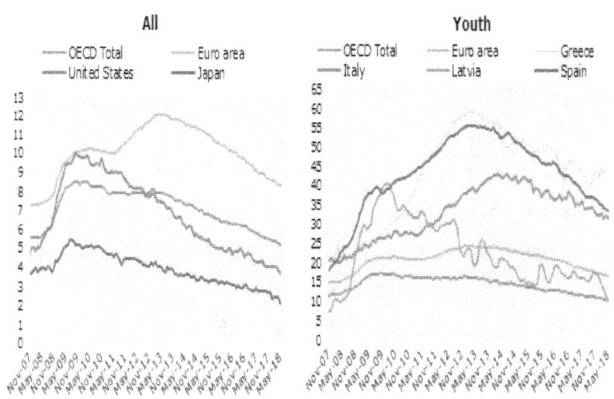
OECD Harmonised Unemployment Rates, s.a.

The central bankers could say that it does not matter what else happened in parallel, once their main goal was achieved. As noted earlier, there has also been an increase in investment in business research and development. At first glance, everything seems to have gone according to the central banks' plan, which was to increase investment to boost employment. The chart below, unfortunately, modifies things somewhat. In this it seems that investments in recent decades are directed to the creation of software and technical equipment and not, so much, to industry and infrastructure. This trend was seen in the previous report on venture capitals. It is no coincidence, then, that capital is invested to technology companies. They just follow a trend that started in the 80's. The reasons for this can be various. The main reason for this seems to be that creating a popular digital platform or software company can generate fast and high profits. But it may also be related to a more general change in the behavior of consumers, who are more interested in experiences in the intangible world of the internet than in the real world. The issue, however, in this case is not that. The point is, investing in software does not create enough jobs. Once some developers create software, the already installed communications network is used, without the need for new employees. The question that arises now is: if new jobs did not emerge from the investments made, where did they come from? Before that, however, we will show how wrong is the prevailing notion that that an increase in investment necessarily leads to an increase in jobs.

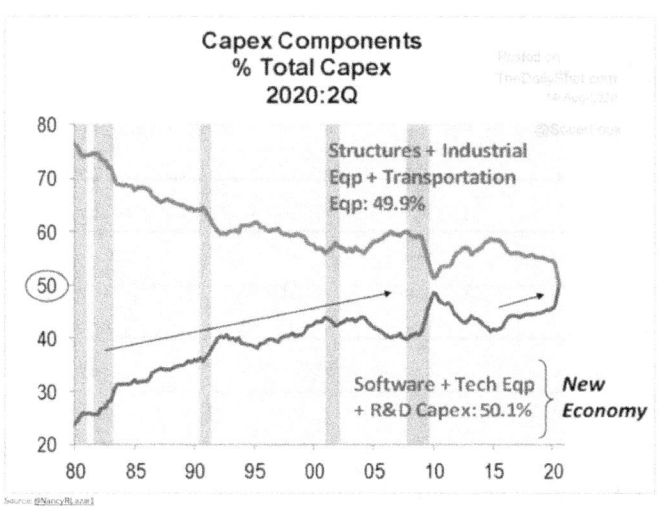

The wrong recipe

Central banks seek, with QE, companies to have a lot of money at their disposal. As we have seen before, they did it after 2008. However, the fact that multinationals have a lot of money does not mean that they will give it to their employees or that they will hire others. No one forces them to do it and they do not do it. What central bankers want is for companies to invest in research and development. As we have seen, they invest more in creating software that does not lead to the creation of many jobs

However, even if it were assumed that all investments were directed to the creation of consumer goods the end result would not be much better. It is true that the creation of new tangible products leads to the development of a new market, in which some new companies would be established that would undertake the continuous manufacture and distribution of the new product, which does not apply in the case of the creation of new software. A software program is made only once and then used by netizens smartphones, while a tangible good needs to be made and distributed on a permanent basis to be available to consumers. The new companies that would undertake the construction and distribution of this good would inevitably hire employees.

We must not forget, however, that at the same time the continuous improvement of production lines results in the need for fewer and fewer workers in production. It was clearly seen in the diagram with the industrial production of the USA. The only case in which investments would create more new jobs would be, if the rate of increase in the discovery of new innovative tangible goods was greater than the rate of decrease in the number of workers needed in the production process. Unfortunately, such a thing is impossible, because even if a product is truly innovative, useful, exciting, etc., it takes some time for a person to get used to it and start consuming it. New product markets are not created, overnight, for reasons due to human psychosynthesis. There is more return to the consumption of old products, than to consumption of new ones. Technologies that improve capital productivity are not subject to such constraints and, at the same time, are favored by existing financial conditions. You see, big companies not only invest in research to create new consumer goods and services, they also invest in robotics, production automation, 3-D printing, etc. That is, they invest in technologies that replace employees. Perhaps ultimately, increasing investment will lead to a reduction in available jobs, contrary to what all bankers, politicians and economists say.

The question, then, remains, where did these new jobs that reduced the global unemployment rate come from? One answer could be that this happened because the unemployment rate does not include those that are unemployed, but they do not intend to look for a new job. Unfortunately, there are many people who belong to the above category and live, either with allowances, or with a pocket money from their parents. This phenomenon is, in fact, particularly intense in Greece. The non-registration of this category as unemployed reduces the unemployment rate. Nevertheless, it cannot adequately justify such a sharp drop in unemployment. In the USA, for example, in 2019 the unemployment rate reached a low of fifty years. Something else must happen in parallel.

How did the central banks drop unemployment?

The irony is that eventually the central banks managed to create new jobs as a result of situations they did not seek to cause and will never admit to causing them. A phenomenon to which the central banks are largely responsible, as explained earlier, and which contributes to reducing unemployment, is to maintain and increase inequality. A large part of the tertiary sector relies on the consumption of wealthy consumers. Thus, with central banks supporting large corporations and the financial sector, this critical mass of consumers continued to exist. And not only did it continue to exist, but after 2008 it strengthened even more. Thus, the demand for special services increased, apart from the conventional ones. The chart below, by the Brookings Institution, shows which occupations were the most sought after in the United States from 2010 to 2017. So it seems that the biggest increase in demand was for manicurists, masseurs, skin care professionals, cooks, people who undertake pet care and personal trainers. It cannot be coincidence that the growing demand for such special services occurred, when the wealth of a very small portion of people skyrocketed. The creation of new jobs, no matter how it came about, is a positive event, but one cannot ignore the fact that these are vulnerable and low-paid jobs. He could say that a new class of 'servants' was created. The increase in demand for the professions mentioned, shows that after 2008 a society was created, without a strong middle class. A society made up of the very rich and those who offer services to them. Once upon a time, those who belonged to the second group would be called servants[19].

At the same time, the central banks, through their actions, helped to maintain two critical groups of employees. The first is those who worked in zombie companies, who did not lose their jobs. As we have shown before, zombie companies have been growing steadily since 2008. Under normal circumstances, those who worked in them would have lost their jobs. The problem is that their salaries are usually low. Companies that are technically supported and maintained due to the easy financing environment set up by central banks, need to appear in society that they are doing everything to survive. So the managers hired, proceed to the easiest solution to reduce their expenses, which is, of course, the reduction of labor costs. Employees in turn accept any reduction in wages and benefits, thinking that this contributes to the survival of their company. It is a pity because the sacrifices of employees are made for nothing, for a show that the system works. In order for the system operators to claim that the bankrupt companies are borrowing, not because of the particular financial environment, but because their prospects improved after the labor cost cuts they made. The central bankers, investors and executives of the zombie companies pretend that the system works, because it benefits them. Central bankers are dropping unemployment figures. Investors who, buy bonds of zombie companies, earn higher returns, without the corresponding risk. Their CEOs continue to enjoy the same standard of living. The only ones who pay for it, are the employees of the zombie companies.

The other critical group of employees who did not lose their jobs were civil servants. According to the Organization for Economic Co-operation and Development (OECD) from 2007 to 2015 its member countries slightly increased public sector employment from 17.9% to 18.1% [20]. It is not a big increase, but the fact that, at the present time, approximately 1 in 5 employees, works in the public sector, remains important. It is doubtful whether tax revenues, without the assistance of central banks in the states, would be enough to pay so many civil servants. The tax revenues of the states in the aforementioned period increased very little. In any case, the central banks, by strengthening the state budgets of all countries by reducing their financing costs, made a significant contribution to preventing the dismissal of civil servants.

So the central banks by making the rich richer and helping the zombie companies and the states not to proceed with layoffs were able to increase employment. However, they were not able to fully restore the labor channel. Overall employee earnings, unfortunately, continued to decline. The second chart below shows that central banks have failed to reverse the downward trend in wages relative to total income. Could this have been avoided?

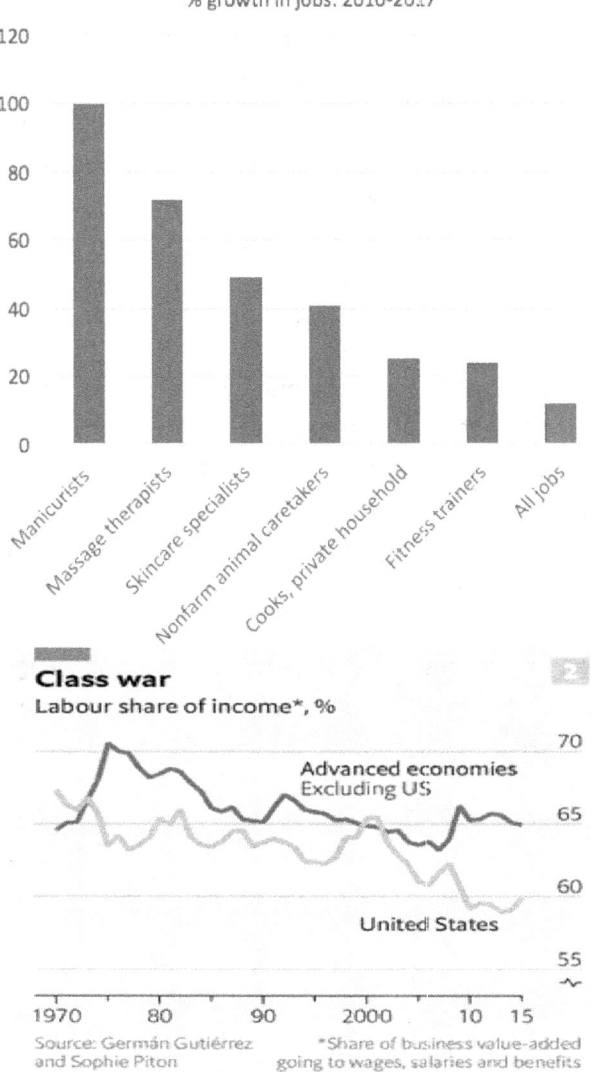

The issue of the minimum wage

At this point we have to see a controversial issue as to whether the state should set the minimum wage. Most economists argue that for no reason should, the minimum wage of an employee, be set. The market must always decide the amount of the salary in order for the companies to remain competitive. Since 2015, however, some U.S. states increased the minimum wage, and employers operating in those states had been forced to pay higher wages to their employees. The results of this action turned out to be anything but catastrophic. Employees received more money without the companies as a whole suffering a reduction in their profits. This increase in the share of labor relative to total income in the USA is shown in the second of the two previous charts. What had happened?

What economists, who reject the increase in the basic wage, are wrong is that they take for granted that the current environment in which businesses operate is that of the free market.[21] This of course is not the case. There are companies that have access, through the issuance of bonds, to money and there are also small and medium companies that do not have. So those who have high cash reserves can increase the salaries of their employees. The fact that they do not have a drop in profits is explained, because the employees with increased wages are at the same time their consumers with a bigger wallet for shopping. So the increase in salaries from companies eventually returns to them. One should not ignore, moreover, that the workers who are mainly favored by the increase of the minimum wage are the low-wage earners, who, whatever they receive as a salary, have no chance of saving it or investing it in the stock exchanges. They would buy goods that they would have liked to buy before, but did not have the money . After all, is the solution to low wages simply to increase them through legislation?

I wish that were the case, but things are not so simple. In America, in recent years, employees employed by large companies have surpassed those employed by small and medium-sized enterprises. The former have access to easy money, while the latter usually do not. Vulnerable small and medium-sized firms cannot easily absorb an increase in labor costs caused by the increase in the minimum wage. As mentioned earlier, these enterprises are often forced to pay low wages to cope with high competition. An imposed increase in their labor costs can lead them to bankruptcy. So in the US, where most people work in large companies, an increase in the basic positive can be implemented with positive results for the wider economy. However, in economies dominated by self-employment and small and medium-sized companies which do not have sufficient funding, a large increase in the minimum wage is very likely to be unenforceable.

In any case, there is a limit to how much the minimum wage can be increased. Each company does not stop looking at its own interest even if, on the whole, an increase in their salaries benefited them. So, when the state forces companies to pay very high wages, each one individually has an incentive to invest more money, which is already at its disposal, in technologies that will replace the workers in production. Thus, if the imposed wage increase exceeds a certain limit, the consequence will be redundancies. Again, technology is the one that not only makes human labor obsolete in the productive process, but also puts a ceiling on wage increases.

Why does the state not save us?

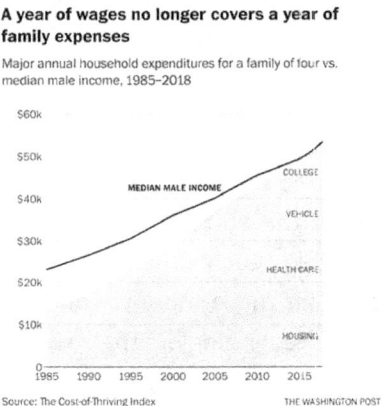

A year of wages no longer covers a year of family expenses

Major annual household expenditures for a family of four vs. median male income, 1985-2018

Source: The Cost-of-Thriving Index   THE WASHINGTON POST

As we have seen from 2008 until the advent of the coronavirus, states in the western world increased their social spending, but while they had the money, they reduced their public investment. Even so, the increase in social spending was limited, without being able to drastically reduce inequality and sufficiently increase the incomes of the low-wage earners. This is clearly shown in the chart above, which shows the median income of a man in the United States, from 1985 to 2015. The median income divides a population into two equal parts. Half have an income above the median and the other half below. It is generally a better indicator of the income of the inhabitants of a country, because it does not take into account the extremes, which are the very rich and the very poor. As it turns out in the USA, the income of an average American in 2015 is not enough to cover the expenses for home, health care, car and college of a family of four, for the first time in history. In other developed economies, the situation may not be so νεγατιωε, but it is still a general rule that an employee's salary is no longer enough to support a family. Why did the states, even if they could, not help their citizens more?

The main constraint faced by the public sector is political. While states have access to large sums of money, they do not make full use of it to avoid greatly increasing public deficits and debt. Normally it should be said that the restriction is fiscal, but it would be wrong. There are, of course, politicians who still believe that high debt is a serious problem. This category, of course, is constantly shrinking. Anyway, we do not know what kind of politician is more dangerous: the one who naively still believes that after all that has happened, high debt is a real problem or the one who cynically adopts the above view for political reasons?

While states usually have a direct connection to central bank money and their debts are skyrocketing, in the public sphere, unfortunately, the orthodox economic thinking survives, which argues that if a state has a high deficit and debt, it risks the future of its citizens. It is an argument that everyone understands because equates the finances of the state with those of the household. Everyone knows that if someone spends more, than he earns, he will end up without money and will not be able to survive. This personal experience of the citizens is used by many politicians to make a career, stating that they are opponents of the high public deficit and debt. The point is that they remember to utter it whenever it suits them. They forget it when low social spending can upset their voters, and they remember it when opinion polls suggest that bringing orthodox economics back to the forefront will give them more votes. It is not necessary for most of the citizens of a country to have a high standard of living in order for the orthodox view to have a high impact, it can be camouflaged and take other forms. The most common form is when some politicians imply or explicitly state that those who receive benefits, increasing the national debt, are immigrants or permanent residents of another nationality. Thus a political message with a racist background is projected under the cloak of orthodox economic thinking.

The previous case is about a politician who has adopted the profile of conservative. However, if a politician adopts the profile of the "man of the people", things will not change much in terms of the amount of social spending. The politician who is in favor of the weak will help them, but up to a point. To the extent that the financially vulnerable, with the benefits they receive from the state, will be able to survive marginally, but not to upgrade their standard of living. Politicians know that if they give them more money, they will take it for granted and will not be grateful to them. They prefer to give so much money to their voters that they consider them their saviors and at the same time accuse their political opponents of preventing them from giving more.

The result is that politicians of all spectrums, tacitly, agree the state to make the same level of social spending in absolute size. That is why all states, after 2008, increased their social expenditures, but in moderation, without fully solving the economic problem of their citizens. They were forced to do so because the decline in the people 's incomes was large due to the labor problem. If they did not increase spending, there would be social unrest. Even the believers of orthodox economic policies would react if the economy collapsed. They would also ask for the intervention of the state. However, it was not in the interest of any politician to make more social expenditures or more public investments.

This informal agreement between the politicians, however, has other negative consequences besides the economic ones. Gradually, the citizens of all countries realize that, whatever party they vote for, nothing will change radically in their economic situation. Everyone knows that no matter what economic changes the politicians promised, the result will again be one of the same: an average economic situation. The voters, from one point onwards, were not excited when the parties were arguing over economic issues. So the politicians, in order to continue to mobilize the crowds, started the identical rhetoric. Political confrontation began to take place on the basis of identities. Even economic policies are viewed in the same perspective. That's why immigration now overshadows the economic problem on the political agenda. Politics turned into a bad-tasting and dangerous show. As long as the field of controversy was at the level of economic policies, the citizens used their logic to vote and were not fanatical. When the field of controversy shifted to what everyone is, politicians turned to the mood of the people. Thus the world is often presented nowadays divided and fanatical.

The recent decline in the quality of democracy in the world[22] and the gradual lifting of a state's limitation on how much it can spend and borrow are not unrelated phenomena. The fiscal constraint also served as a constraint on state power. Now, because of the central banks, politicians use fiscal restraint as a means of communication, without really restricting them. As long as it existed, at least the rulers were required to be serious and responsible, to a degree. They should draw up and follow an economic plan. A good politician is now only one who handles communication tactics well. That is, the better the liar, the better. Unfortunately, all this is not reflected in economic indicators. The QE effects are much more insidious and long-term.

So far, reference has been made to the fact that budget constraint is used as a political tool in the political game of a parliamentary democracy. But what if a politician thinks a little more cunningly? If he thinks, for example, to use the free money, not only to get rich (which is the least), but to stay in power permanently. If he suddenly realizes that he is no longer limited by the market restrictions , which would require the state to pay attention to its expenses and revenues. How would he use the abundant money to stay in power?

He would initially bribe those officials who held key positions to legitimize his regime. He would, of course, give a lot of money to the police and the army to protect him. He would form a narrow circle of cronies. Every regime, however, needs some popular support to last a long time. In this hypothetical scenario, the wannabe dictator has infinite money at his disposal. How could he make better use of it? To distribute the money generously to the people of his country, without any restrictions? No. Every self-respecting power has something that the subjects do not have and provides it little by little to continue to control them. Our hero would keep his people in poverty and give them so much money that in their eyes he would be their messiah.

It is obvious that in all cases no politician is willing to give so much money to the world that the losses of the labor channel are fully compensated. The absolute criterion of both the dictator and the conventional politician is to give, so much so that, marginally, social unrest is avoided. But this is the least. What's worse is that the money of the central banks is slowly replacing the money that different regimes earned from the exploitation of oil, consolidating their power. Every wannabe dictator gains access to a money tree, which he can use to cling to power. As we have seen, borrowing costs have fallen not only in developed economies but also in emerging ones.

One could say that this can only happen in countries with weak democratic institutions. That is, in countries that have only emerging economies and not developed ones. But this is not the case. The danger may not be immediate, but a ruler of a developed country can gradually erode democratic institutions with the help of the abundant money at his disposal. He may not be able to bribe all the government officials for the simple reason that they are already rich, but he can use the money to increase his popularity. After all, didn't Trump, the president of the USA, do the same? Since taking office, Trump skyrocketed America's deficits and debt. Since he could, why not do it anyway? And all this while leading the Republican Party, which had always been against high deficits and high public debt. As if by magic, everything was forgotten when Republicans found that they could satisfy their voters using Fed money. In this case, the rich ones. The deficit in the US budget, from tax cuts to wealthy citizens and businesses, which was considered Trump's biggest reform, was covered by the Fed's purchases of government bonds. In addition, when the coronavirus came, Trump was fighting with his political opponents about who will give the most money to American citizens. On the one hand, he was accusing Democrats that would turn America into Venezuela, on the other hand, he had no problem handing out a checks with his name on to American citizens. Even if the US economy was hit by the coronavirus pandemic, Trump was considered by

American citizens to be, by the end, more capable of managing the economy than Biden. In the end, of course, Trump lost the election and did not overthrow American democracy, but degraded it considerably. In all his efforts he had the help of the US central bank. All this shows that the worst thing, in the long run, is not that politicians do not use the money of central banks adequately. What is worse is that politicians gain more power, which may undermine democracy, to the detriment of our freedom.

Finally, reference should be made to a popular narrative of the events that took place in 2008 and beyond, as to the role of states, which, however, completely distorts the truth[23]. The story goes like this: 'In 2008, some bad bankers gave a lot of loans to poor people, who could not repay them, with the result that the banks, along with some multinationals, risked bankruptcy. The states, then, borrowed a lot to save the banks and the multinationals. So in the years that followed, the states, in order to repay the previous loans, imposed austerity.' The above narrative is very insidious, because it quotes true facts, mixed with false ones. Again, the trick used to distort the truth is to use the orthodox economic thinking .Viewed from this perspective, the above narrative makes sense. But there are two lies. One small and one large. The small is that, as we saw after 2008, the states as a whole may not increased their spending as much as they should, but they did not impose austerity. The big lie is that even if we accept that they imposed austerity, it was not because of the high debts, but because the governments of the states chose it. Essentially, the above tale presents the state as the victim, who was submitted to the capital, which, in this case, are the banks and the multinationals, having no other choice. Even if this is circulated, mainly, by 'left' politicians to say their stories about the bloodthirsty capitalists etc, it is also accepted by other politicians. This is because it presents the latter as responsible, who after rescuing the financial system, then took care to repay the debts of the state.

Almost none of the above, of course, applies. The greatest distortion of the facts is achieved, not with the two lies that are reported, but with what is omitted. In this narrative no reference is made to the central banks. As if they do not exist, while nowadays, no reference can be made to the financial markets, without emphasizing the central role of central banks. If it mentioned them, it should have said that the central banks in 2008 created money and gave it to the states to save some banks and multinationals. The printing of money, however, did not stop then, but continued after 2008. The states had the money to adequately increase their social spending. They, for their own reasons, chose not to do so. As we have seen, QE, in any case, consists mainly of purchase of government bonds. The states are the main institutions that are favored by the money printing of the central banks. It is absurd to say that bankers and multinationals took advantage of the innocent states when they are the most important financial market players. And if we have to say, who is most responsible for the low incomes of the people after 2008: the states or the multinationals and the banks. Then we would say states, because the other bodies are not obliged to help the people, while the governments of the states are elected to do so.

Final report

Having said all this, it is still difficult to draw a final conclusion whether the adoption of money printing as the official policy of the central banks of developed countries has had positive or negative consequences in the world. Various studies by economists have shown that it has had positive consequences. Maybe they are right. It is true that inequality increased and the state gained too much power, but the money, which was eventually channeled into the real economy, was beneficial. Even if most of the money ended up in the pockets of the rich and in the stock markets, the little money that managed to escape , helped the vulnerable workers in the service sector.

Nevertheless, it remains a fact that QE arose by chance. It all relied on the simplistic logic of printing as much money as possible, so that some of it manage to reach the most vulnerable citizens. As long as inflation did not rise, central banks could do it. Finally, from 2008 to 2020, inflation never appeared on the horizon, so the central banks of developed countries printed money almost throughout this period. Look at what Fed President Ben Bernanke said in 2010, two years after the crisis: 'A more relaxed credit policy will stimulate economic growth. For example, lower mortgage rates will make it easier to get a home and allow more homeowners to refinance their mortgages. Lower interest rates on corporate bonds will encourage investment. And higher stock prices will increase the wealth of the consumer, will help him increase his self-confidence, which will boost his consumption. Increased consumption will lead to increased incomes and profits, which in a virtuous circle, will support economic growth[24]. '

He looks very happy, marginally excited. Without any shame and with smugness he lists the positives of the 'loose credit policy' in 2010, while two years ago, he had said that it was an extraordinary measure. It has suddenly become a permanent measure, which has a lot of positive consequences. Initially he states that the citizens will get new mortgage loans. Eventually, only a few new loans were given. Those who already had mortgages, it is true that they were favored because interest rates were not increased. This does not mean, of course, that they did not continue to be in debt to the banks and financially ruined. Business investment, as we have seen, increased, but without creating many new jobs . As for the virtuous circle he mentions, it is more about the circular rise of the stock markets and not the consumption. It should, of course, be credited to Ben Bernanke that he admits that, because of QE, the value of the shares is rising. Central bankers usually do not admit it. The cycle simply goes as described before. It is: rise in the value of shares → increase in income → new rise in shares. It is not: rise in the value of shares → increase in income → increase in self-confidence → increase in consumption → increase in corporate profits → new increase in income. This is because the shares, as we have shown, are owned by the rich and most of the additional income resulting from the increase in the value of their shares returns to the stock market, because they cannot consume much more. It is true, however, that sometimes from their great joy, because they become even richer without doing anything, they demand special services , giving work to those who offer them. Maybe in the end, Ben Bernanke was right, and the central banks creating a new class of servants to the rich, saved the world economy after 2008. In 2020, Covid-19 made its appearance.

The age of free Money

Coronavirus and free money

And while central banks were printing money 12 years after the mortgage crisis, patiently waiting for inflation to rise in order to withdraw the emergency measures of 2008, the coronavirus made its appearance. This time, it was as if they had been ready for a long time. No, because they had devised a special action plan in case something happened, but because, after 2008, they had learned that market intervention did not lead to inflation. So they did what they knew best: they bought almost everything on the financial market, without hesitation and without limit. In other words, they continued to do what they did: print money. What changed was that they did it on an even larger scale. To be precise, much bigger. As you can see, in the first of the following charts, the balance sheets of the major central banks in a few days jumped to 20 trillion, about the size of the US GDP, the world's largest economy. The intervention they had made in

2008 pales in comparison to that of 2020. They bought not only government, but also, corporate bonds. The central bank that intervened the most was again the Fed. Again it set up US dollar channels to all countries that needed US dollars. (swaps). The most interesting fact, however, is shown in the second diagram. Not only the central banks of developed economies but also many central banks of the developing ones bought government bond with newly created cash. We see, for example, that the central banks of Philippines, Indonesia, Ghana, Chile, India, South Africa, Poland and Croatia bought their government bonds. This huge intervention of the central banks prevented the collapse of the stock exchanges and offered support to the two pillars of the system, but led, as expected, to the known side effects, which we will examine later.

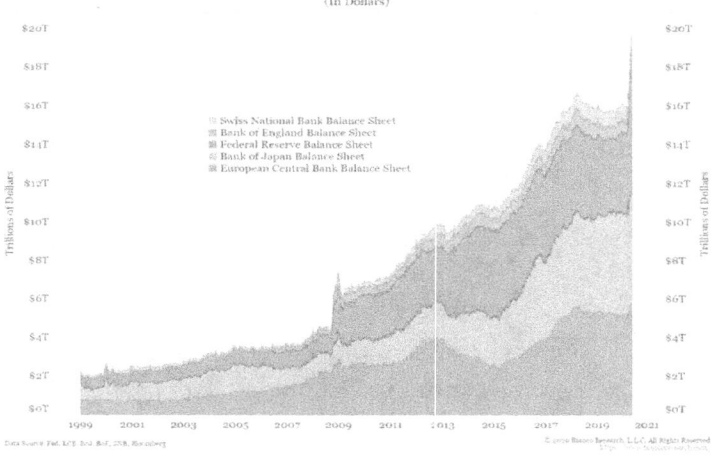

Cumulative Central Bank Balance Sheets
(In Dollars)

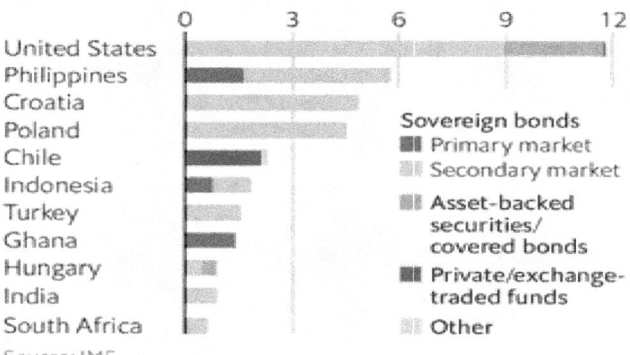

Shopping expeditions
Central-bank asset purchases, % of GDP
Mar-Aug 2020

Source: IMF

The Economist

The markets followed their own path

Markets, after a sharp decline, soon returned to their upward trajectory. To be precise, very soon. While all economists have acknowledged that humanity was experiencing its greatest post-war recession, stock markets were in another reality. The S&P 500, the main US index, in the 2008 crisis took about 5.5 years to make new highs, this time about 6 months were enough. The chart below shows the S&P 500 in relation to the profits of the companies it includes. Although the gap between corporate profits and their share prices widens from 2015 to 2020, at least they have followed the same direction. In 2020, that changed: corporate profits plunged as their stock market prices soared, after a slight drop. The complete disconnection of the markets in relation to the real economy was a fact.

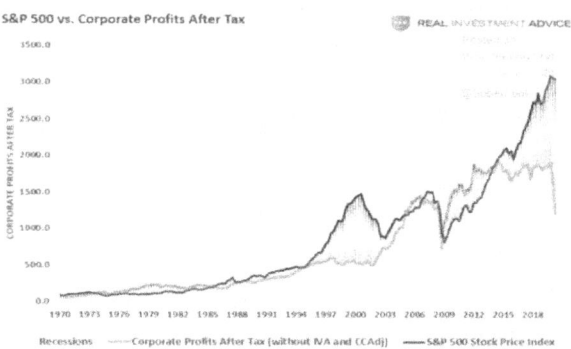

The biggest miracles, however, did not happen in the stock market, but in the bond market, which is the most important, because it is the main way of channeling money to companies and states. Until central bank intervention in 2020, when the global economy was in deep recession, companies usually could not sell bonds, and if they did, they would have to pay a high coupon. Here, defying all economic logic, the average corporate bond coupon fell below 2% for the first time, while corporate debt made a new record high. All this is shown in the first of the following charts. This happens when there is a buyer with infinite money who guarantees that he will buy all the bonds regardless of the fundamentals of companies .

The miracles in the bond market do not stop here. What happened in the government bond market also offers a glimpse into the future. As can be seen in the second chart, the size of government bonds issued by the US, the EU, the UK and Japan has risen sharply as expected. One would expect a sharp increase in the volume of government bonds in private portfolios, but it seems that not only did they not increase, but they also decreased slightly. What does this mean? It means that for the first time in history, government debt was bought almost entirely by central banks. By 2020, central banks were buying mainly government bonds to allay fears of private investors so that they too could start buying. In 2020, the world's major central banks bought almost all the government bonds issued by their countries, without the participation of private investors. The central bankers say, as always, that this was an emergency measure, which will be withdrawn later. However, they do not become credible when they said the same in 2008. Maybe in the future the states will be financed directly by the central banks. The end result of this inconceivable intervention was that in 2020 over 70% of global debt, government and corporate, was serviced at an interest rate below 1%. We are talking about a flood of money. We are officially in the age of free money, that is, the money that is created, out of thin air, by the central banks.

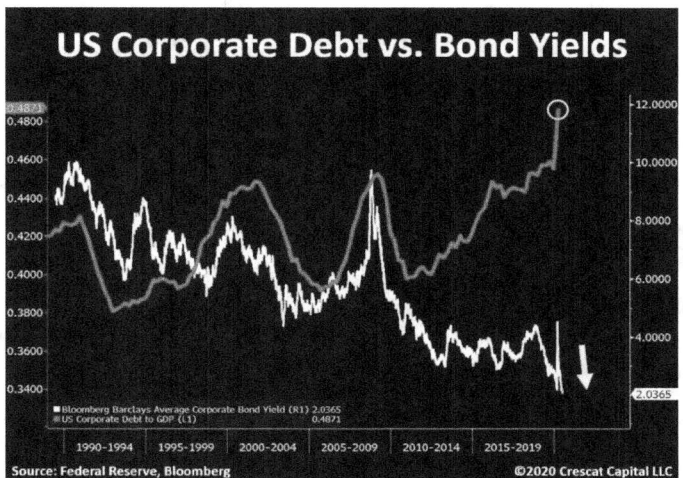

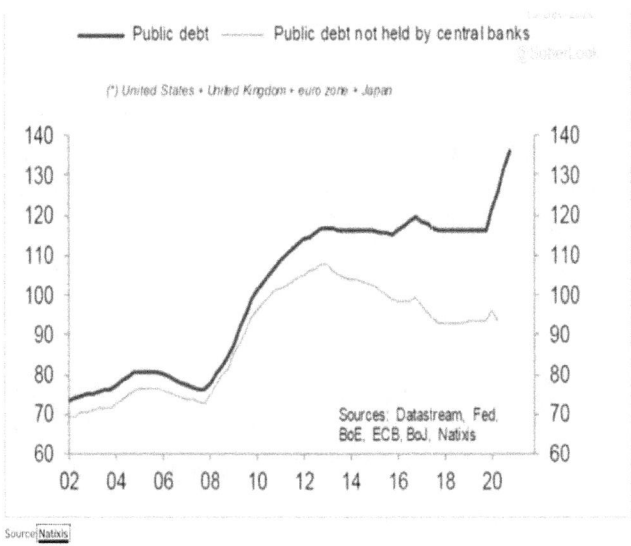

Theoretically, the reason central banks support the market is to channel money fairly into the two pillars of the system. Ultimately they support the market to support the wider society. The market is the means and not the end. Even if there were, in the beginning, good intentions, the central banks, now with the interventions, operate mainly for the benefit of the financial markets. It would be the paradise that John Law had dreamed of.

The pattern of the market not only change, but is reversed. The investor who behaves prudently and has a plan is not rewarded, but the one who is reckless and acts instinctively. The perfect reversal.

In the end, the prudent investor is forced to adapt to the new situation. Central banks have eliminated the risk from the markets. No one is punished for being too gambler. Normally the return and risk of a financial product are inversely proportional. One might have made more money at one time, but at the same time risked losing more money than investing in safer financial products. Now everyone knows that no one will lose their money, so everyone is committed to buying what is most risky to earn more.

The coronavirus was a buying opportunity, because there were some who behaved like normal people and sold their shares and bonds, anticipating the recession that would follow. They were not wrong, but that matters little. Most investors knew that the central banks would intervene, as they did, and they rushed to buy what was sold. Any serious geopolitical event that happens, from now on, on the planet will be considered a buying opportunity. It is possible that the human race is in danger of extinction and the stock markets will rise.

The complete reversal that exists in the way the market operates was reflected in the most brilliant way in the bond market. When the price of bonds increases, their yield falls. Investors, of course, want their bond to have as high a return as possible. Normally higher returns are associated with greater risk. This is no longer the case. Investors did not buy government bonds because they were afraid. They did not buy them because they were not afraid at all. They knew they would have zero or negative yields, so they chose to buy bonds with higher yields. Let's say, 'junk' bonds that carry higher risk of default. The result was that central banks were forced to buy all of their government bonds. At the same time, huge demand for corporate bonds plunged their yields to record lows. Market players behave like spoiled kids, whose central banks satisfy all their wishes.

Bankers and venture capitalists became even richer

I think you remember when we said that venture capitals had shares in start-ups, which had high valuations, but only on paper. Until the advent of the coronavirus, investors were reluctant to list their start-ups on the stock exchange, fearing that they would lose value. In 2020 this changed. The central banks have created the ideal conditions so that the firms that went public were the most in the last 20 years, as shown in the chart below. Most companies, of course, did not make a profit, but that did not bother any investor. Everyone was betting on their future prospects, which seemed bright because of the pandemic. The scenario that emerged was that technology companies were favored because of the lockdowns that were imposed in many countries, resulting in many human activities being done online. That was true, but it does not in any way justify this buying frenzy of all kinds of tech companies that only had losses on their balance sheets. The real reason so many companies listed on the world's stock exchanges was the relentless pursuit of investors for even higher returns. They, just, bet on the winning horse. So many venture capitalists were rewarded generously even if they were putting money into loss-making companies, that offered nothing to society. At the same time, banks had the most revenues from commissions over the last 20 years, due to the issuance of so many bonds and shares. It would be a pity, after all, for the favorite children of the system to be absent from the party.

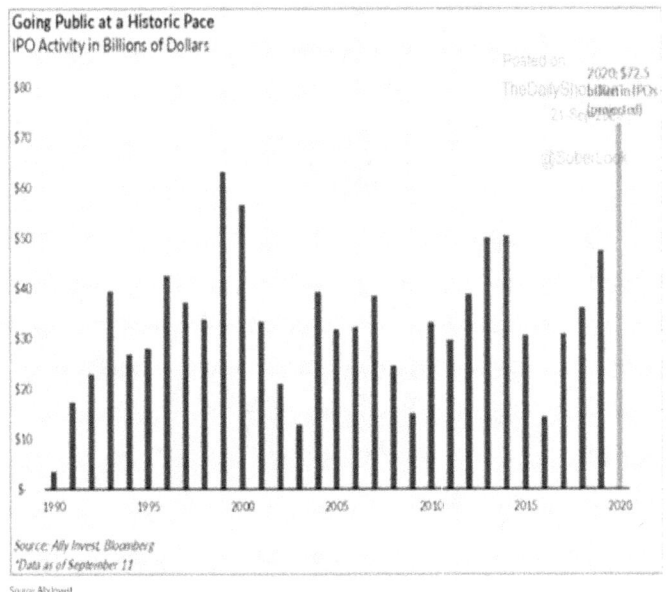

The labor channel collapsed.

From the fancy world of stock markets and unicorns we move on to the real world of work. There, unfortunately, things did not go so well. As expected, services were most affected, which, as mentioned, is the sector that employs the most employees. Worse still, the pandemic hit the low-paying professions hardest. Those working in tourism, catering, nightclubs/bars and retail suffered the most. All the above-mentioned occupations have in common that they presuppose the physical contact between the employee and the client, which was their Achilles heel with the advent of the virus.

If the blow to service sector is short-lived and everything comes back to normal, when, at some point, Covid-19 stops bothering humanity, it will be fine. Unfortunately, there is a high chance that the virus that has hit the tertiary sector will have a more permanent character. This sector is based on the habit of man to leave home to shop, have fun, meet friends, eat etc. To meet these human needs, the respective businesses have been set up, such as restaurants, bars, cafes, cinemas, etc. This is how most companies in the tertiary sector survive. This model works mainly in cities, where there are more people and therefore customers. The only thing for sure is that it cannot work if people sit at home, where they will eat, work, watch series and movies and go shopping. This is what most people on the planet did because of the lockdowns that had been imposed. When the coronavirus disappears completely, it is not certain that the habits created during the pandemic will disappear overnight. Specifically two trends are very likely to survive.

The first trend is online shopping. Retail is more at risk than any other industry[1]. Even before the pandemic, online shopping was growing every year. It is very likely that the virus has dealt the final blow to small shops and malls, with the corresponding negative effects on employment. The second trend, which has developed since the virus appeared, is much more dangerous and insidious. We refer to work from home. Many companies have found that many jobs can be done remotely without having to pay for business trips and office space rentals. The employees, to the surprise of their bosses, were more productive, for the most part, when they worked from home. At the same time, they stated that they already preferred it[2]. After all this, it is certain that remote work has come to stay. Many companies have already announced that they will continue to apply this practice later.

Those who can work remotely are usually paid above average and are the best customers, as mentioned, of city stores. If, even a small number of them, work permanently remotely from their beautiful countryside homes, the consequences can be catastrophic for many businesses in the cities. If what everyone in the world knows, that there are more job opportunities in the city ceases to be valid, unemployment will reach unimaginable levels. Those who claim that the lost jobs of the cities will be replaced with new ones in the countryside are not right. If some city dwellers are scattered throughout the universe, many urban businesses will not be able to survive and rural clientele will not grow enough to make new countryside businesses sustainable.

The response of the states

The states, with the help of the central banks, reacted immediately. Government assistance went either to businesses or directly to the people. In the EU, governments covered the payroll costs of companies affected by the pandemic in the first months. Unemployment benefits were given to those who lost their jobs in the United States. In all countries, aid to small and medium-sized enterprises was provided in one way or another. State aid was, in fact, unprecedented and would not have been possible without the purchase of government bonds by central banks. But is the huge state intervention enough to fully heal the coronavirus wounds?

The public sector constraints on financial support for society that existed after 2008 and that we described earlier still apply today. In the face of a tragic event that has happened to humanity, politicians of all spectrums agreed to take emergency action. In such cases, the orthodox economic view is always set aside, because it does not benefit anyone. Suddenly, there is money. As time goes on, however, the arguments in the public debate about the high deficits and debts that will have to be collected, will begin again.

Government debt worldwide, however, is so high that it will never be repaid. State tax revenues are not enough in any case. In Western societies, the population is shrinking, with the result that economic growth is declining. Tax revenues will inevitably have a similar course. Research shows that the more women are educated and involved in the workforce, the fewer children they have. It is a positive development that should not be considered as negative.

The debate over high debt will continue only for partisan reasons. There are, of course, some financial analysts and economists who expect high debts to lead to the revelation they have been waiting for decades. Let them wait a few more decades. When high debts do not sound good, other ways to report them will be found. It is already being discussed not to use the quotient of the national debt to the GDP of the country as an indicator of the debt, but the cost of servicing the debt to the GDP[3]. If this is done, government debt will be zero overnight, because we live in the age of free money, when the majority of government debt is serviced at zero or negative interest rates. But no matter how the debt is measured, the golden rule of all kinds of politicians will not change, which is that government spending will be at a level where people, marginally, will not become so outraged that they will revolt.

What will be left, unfortunately, will be the politicians' access to free money. Getting a taste, leaders of the world will want more. They will take advantage of it to increase, even more, their influence in our lives. Somewhere here, however, the reference to politicians must stop, because this time the responsibility for dealing with the economic effects of the pandemic lies equally, if not more, with the central bankers.

The coronavirus as a tipping point

Always, in times of crisis, criticism focuses on politicians. In the Covid-19 pandemic we should focus on central bankers. People either do not know the crucial role they play in dealing with crises, or they believe them when they claim to have done what they could, which means they printed infinite money. They behave as if they paid out of their pocket. They are always hiding behind the backs of politicians, but in 2020 the spotlight had to fall on them.

In 2008 it could be accepted that they intervened in the market and saved the big companies so that the sell-off would not be generalized and the credibility of the financial system would not be questioned. Thus, a major recession was averted which would lead to the poverty of many inhabitants of the planet. The continuation of their intervention in the markets with QE, marginally, could be accepted. They may have caused a sharp rise in inequality and wages continued to fall, but at least they reduced unemployment. In 2020 things were different. They can no longer claim that they did not know the side effects of their policy. The moment when the rich, comfortably in their villas or on their private islands, see their fortunes soar in the markets, while a large number of workers in the tertiary sector lose their jobs, reflects, in all its glory, the inequality which is caused by central banks..

With their huge intervention in the market, the stock market indices soared, making even richer its already rich players. This, once again, was seen as the necessary action to get the money to companies and states. 12 years was not enough to understand that companies do not give their money to employees and that the state cannot increase its social spending from one point onwards? What will happen to all these dollars, euro, etc. that were printed? Money cannot stay stagnant, it must be channeled somewhere. It will again end up in the pockets of a few, further increasing inequality. Humanity will be divided into two categories. On the one hand there will be those who have a direct or indirect relationship with the free money of the central banks and on the other hand there will be those who do not have. The second category will barely survive.

We have the right to demand a better solution than that anyway. A solution that does not include the stage where the rich get richer. The man with his ingenuity has reached the moon. Can't bankers with so many postdoctoral degrees think of something better? They had 12 whole years to work out a better crisis plan and presented one of the same. The only thing that changed was that they printed even more money. We cannot believe that they are fools. They are just comfortable with the situation and do not want to change. Why do they want to change something anyway? They enjoy prestige, money and at the same time, many consider them saviors of humanity. They sit at the same table as the CEOs of the multinationals and the leaders of the developed countries, to whom , by chance, they channel free money.

In 2020 a tipping point was reached, because for the first time in history the negative side effects of

QE outweigh its positive effects on society. The further creation of money and its channeling from the existing network, will worsen the situation each time. The problem remains: how will money be channeled to people when the traditional channel of labor is not enough and its situation worsens with each new crisis? The action of the central banks is now making things worse. What is, perhaps, even worse is that the deterioration of the situation is not easily understood so that there is a reaction on our part. Now, with the benefits we enjoy from the states, backed by the central banks, we are just surviving and accepting the situation. We are in danger of falling into mud, from which we will not be able to get out easily. Below we will see some of the solutions that have been proposed.

Suggested solutions

The Chinese model

As we have seen before, Western countries after 2008, while having the money, reduced their investment in infrastructure. The main reason is, as mentioned, the informal agreement between politicians on the amount of government spending. It can also be related to the malfunction and bureaucracy of the public sector. Regardless of the reasons for this, from 2020, calls for more active involvement of the state in the economic life of each country, began to increase. If the private sector cannot create jobs, they say, let the state create them. They argue that the mistake of the western states, which was to reduce their public investment after 2008, should not be repeated. Before we see if this can be a solution, let's look at the case of China. This country, in addition to soon becoming the world's largest economic power, is intervening in the economy in the most efficient way. In essence, the country is the model for those who propose as a solution to the economic problem the more active participation of the state in the economy. China follows a model of state capitalism, but because it is so special, it could be better described as the 'Chinese model'.

In the 1990s, large western companies, aided by the governments of their countries , managed to make China[1] accessible to western capital and China began to trade with the rest of the world. Of course, it had not become a free economy, let alone a liberal democracy, but everyone expected that sooner or later that would happen. Everyone was convinced that an economy in which market laws do not apply, but is controlled by a central body, in which case the Chinese Communist Party (CCP), could not survive. It would suffer like the economy of former Soviet Union. Thus, either, gradually, its economy would become freer, or it would collapse. In the end, none happened. On the contrary, China became a global superpower with a centrally controlled economy. How and why goes beyond the scope of this book, but it is an example of how often erroneous estimates are made by experts

China has a kind of state capitalism. The lives of all citizens are controlled and monitored by the CCP. It has full control of the banks (including the central bank) and most of its companies. Even large non-state-owned companies are required to have CCP members on their boards. It exercises a kind of human resource management over them [2]. The CCP decides in which sectors it will invest and China's regions have specific economic growth goals to achieve each year. As for the financing of all its projects, at least, China does not say that its central bank is politically independent. The central government orders banks to lend wherever it wishes. Banks usually have money to lend to as Chinese citizens, unlike Westerners, are more inclined to save. Of course, state-owned banks have the support of their central bank, which, like all central banks in the world, can create money and give it to them.

The main goal of China is to pull its citizens out of poverty. This is a grandiose goal, because we are talking about a country where in the 1990s almost everyone was poor and because the Chinese make up about one-fifth of the world's population. China does not like the policy of distributing benefits to its citizens to increase their income. The Chinese have to work hard to make money. Thus, China has taken on the colossal task of finding jobs for nearly 1.5 billion people.

It has the largest industrial facilities in the world and exports most of the products in the world. The growing industrial and service sectors, as the Chinese middle class grows, cover the majority of jobs in China. The problem with the industrial sector is that over time it needs fewer human hands and is directly dependent on the demand for goods from the rest of the world, especially America. The demand for goods decreases when there are global crises. In general, Americans have to consume in order for the Chinese to work, who do not consume much. As for the services sector, it is always the weakest in an economy. To address this, the Chinese leadership is investing heavily in infrastructure. In other words, the Chinese are doing what those, who want to increase public investments in the western states, envision..

China's infrastructure investment is growing steadily and growing even more as other sectors of its economy shrink. That is, they build ports, roads, bridges, airports, hydroelectric dams, electricity factories, etc. Even completely new cities. In the first, from the two charts below, it appears that investment in infrastructure is steadily increasing and in the second, its sharp increase in 2008 to address the US mortgage crisis.

The Chinese leadership's obsession with finding work, by all means, for its citizens reaches extreme levels. In order to have economic growth and not have unemployment, they do not hesitate in the face of anything. They have no moral hesitation in expelling their citizens from their villages and transport them to newly built cities. And all this in order to create some more jobs and their provinces to present better economic figures to the central administration.[3] They make as many roads, bridges, houses, etc. as needed so that all Chinese have jobs.

It does not matter that the these projects are not needed and will not be needed in the future, because China's population is also declining.

After what has been said, it does not seem strange that the country that dealt most effectively with the shock of the pandemic was China After initially imposing draconian measures, which its citizens complied with, to curb the virus, it then resorted to its well-known tactic: constructions that no one needs. The funny thing is that its central bank did not have to print a lot of money to finance its new projects. What happened? China issued government bonds, but they were bought by Western investors[4]. Following the logic that 'we put our money in the bonds that offer the highest yields without caring about anything else'. They did so because Chinese government bonds offered a few percentage points higher yields than western bonds. Maybe in the economic and political press, everyone was talking about cold relations between the West and China, but the capital did not care. Thus, China pretended to be in favor of free markets and financed its plans with the money of others . Of course, this does not cease to be a temporary phenomenon. Chinese bonds will soon offer zero yields, as do bonds of all developed economies Chinese officials may have laughed at the naivete of the West, but they too will soon be forced to finance their major projects with printed money. This is the natural end of the story when central banks buy government bonds. Increased demand for Chinese government bonds will gradually reduce their yields. Once this is done, Western funds will stop being buyers, looking for other bonds that offer higher yields. Then the Chinese central bank will be forced to intervene and buy them itself. This is just another incident, which could only happen in the age of free money.

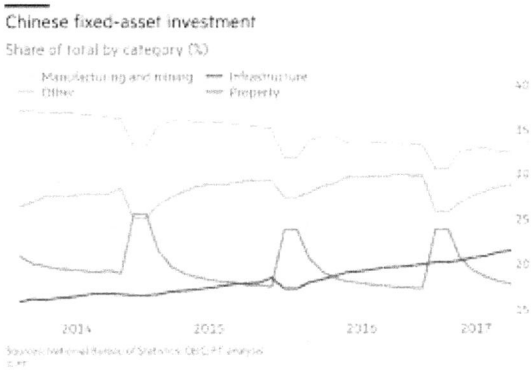

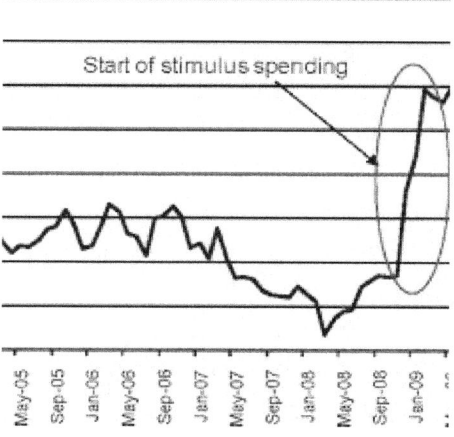

The Chinese state's extreme behavior shows the limits that exist in terms of the efficiency of public investment. However, the solution proposed by the governments of the major western countries in 2020 is to adopt the Chinese model. The EU will set up a recovery fund, as it calls it, 750 billion, to invest in the infrastructure of European countries, with an emphasis on environmentally friendly investments. Similar investments are being prepared by the newly elected US government in 2020 and the United Kingdom[5]. First of all, we can observe that, while a few years ago everyone praised the positives of the free economy and asked China to follow, now the roles have been reversed and all the big western countries want to adopt the Chinese model, which it is essentially a kind of state capitalism.

Beyond that, investments in the infrastructure of western countries need to be made and should have already been made. The responsibility lies with the governments of the western states that for so many years did not maintain, at least, the existing infrastructure. It would be positive to give a boost to investments in green energy. Public investment is positive for society when infrastructure is inadequate and in need of maintenance. At the same time, however, they have a ceiling that was seen, when we referred to the Chinese model. Investments in infrastructure must be made to the extent that they benefit the society . Beyond this point, the environment is simply destroyed, for no real reason. The state should not get to the point of doing projects solely to create jobs. With all the corruption and bribery that accompanies the whole process. The permanent adoption of a system of state capitalism, moreover, is dangerous to the freedom of citizens. It is no coincidence that it applies in China, where everything is controlled by the central government.

Having said the above and speaking on practical level, the state can, by actively intervening in the economic life of each country, completely repair the labor channel. It will be a state that will be financed directly by its central bank and will create jobs in the Greek way (appointment of civil servants) or in the Chinese way or a combination of the two. By appointing civil servants and doing unnecessary projects , a state can effectively fight unemployment. The technology that makes possible to produce goods with minimal human presence, also makes possible the of state capitalism to survive. If one has no problem living in a society dominated by corruption, hypocrisy and, most likely, the suppression of freedom of expression, then state capitalism is the right regime for him. A regime that will create unnecessary new jobs in which, when employees do not pretend to work, they will work making life difficult for others with the bureaucratic hurdles they pose or at the expense of the environment. But I think it would be better to find another solution.

Financial solutions

The first solution that the Fed tried during the pandemic was to set full-time employment as its official goal, without bothering it at the same time if inflation rises.[6] Theoretically until now it wanted growth without inflation, while, with the new measure, FED is willing to accept a period when there will be inflation, without being interested in fighting it. In essence, they say in the markets, again, that they will print dollars as if there is no tomorrow, hoping that prices will start rising again. The problem is, they have been doing this for over ten years and inflation is not coming. Printing even more money will not change anything. They want the economy to overheat ,in order to eventually raise interest rates and stop printing money. In other words, they want a return to the conventional monetary policy, which, however, is a thing of the past.

Others suggest the full adoption of negative interest rates . It is something that the Swiss central bank has implemented [7]. If this were the case all over the world anyone, who made a deposit in a bank, would withdraw less money later. The rationale for adopting the measure is that people should not leave their money inactive in the bank, but either spend it or invest it. In theory, in both cases there would be an increase in economic activity. Essentially, however, what is happening today is going to happen again . Those who do not have a lot of money would spend it anyway. As for the rich, they would invest in the markets to earn more. The only thing that would probably change is that, because no one would leave their money in the bank, the market bubble would become even bigger. The disconnection of the market with the real economy would be beyond imagination.

We need to add something else here. Those who propose the adoption of negative interest rates fear that people will accumulate their money in the form of banknotes and hide it, canceling their 'brilliant' plan. So, to rule out this possibility, they have thought of something. When you hear that central banks are thinking of introducing digital currencies, they open the way for the imposition of negative interest rates[8] They want every citizen to have a digital wallet, something like bank deposits, but which will be under the jurisdiction of the central bank. Banks will be bypassed, this time, completely. They envision a society where no cash will be used at all and in the digital wallet of every citizen they will be able impose, directly, whatever interest rate they want. Specifically negative. So unlike the conventional wallet that remains the same cash, if you do not use it, the money that would be in the digital, would lose value as long as it remained unused. It is understood that if the central banks take such a measure, those with little money will be disproportionately affected. We hope that the central banks will not dare to take such an extreme measure, because they will be afraid of social reactions. Until now, they are hiding behind the backs of politicians, if they literally enter our wallet, they will come out of obscurity and the criticism against them will be intense.

MMT

Another theory that promises solutions and has a lot of buzz is the modern monetary theory (MMT) [9]. According to MMT, a state can finance its economy through the country's banking system until full employment is achieved , without budgetary constraints. The only limitation is inflation. If inflation rises the state will raise taxes and issue government bonds to curb it. They claim that the tax increase will slow down the economy, while the sale of government bonds will reduce the amount of money circulating in the market. Both of these measures are deflationary. A key difference from conventional fiscal policy is that government bonds will not be used as a financing tool, because the state will have as much money as it wants from its central bank anyway. All this sounds good, but again, in essence, nothing changes from the already implemented policy, where government bonds are used as a means of financing. In both cases the central bank creates money from thin air and gives it to the state. In both cases, the state is considered the appropriate body to repair the economy. And finally, both conventional and MMT economists expect inflation, which never comes. However, do not tell them that they are similar because they will be offended. People have more serious problems than dealing with their ideological conflicts.

That said, MMT theorists are moving in the right direction, and at least they are not hypocrites to demonize the money printing , unlike conventional economists who adopt it, but with a heavy heart and always claim that it will be a temporary measure. However, the proposed mechanism does not cease to be a reflection of the existing one. The public and banking sectors are already heavily funded without drastically tackling the economic problem for the reasons mentioned above.

Basic income

As long as the money does not reach the pockets of the citizens through the existing channels, a basic income could be set for all citizens, without conditions.[10] This is a proposal that has been known for a long time. We do not need special arguments to support why in modern society it is necessary for every citizen to have a basic income. It is almost self-evident. In a world where those who are considered 'lucky' because they find work, it is very likely that they will not even cover their basic expenses with their salary, the need for an income for everyone without exception is obvious.

The problems start when the 'progressive' economists who propose the basic income, refer to the thorny issue of its financing. In the age of free money, where central banks directly finance the states, they have been completely cut off from reality and they do not even refer to the financing of basic income through the issuance of government bonds. They take it for granted that the measure will be financed exclusively by taxes.

Economists continue to act as if they do not see the huge elephant in the room, which is nothing more than financing the lion's share of public spending with money freshly printed by central banks. The main reason they do this is because if they did not , there would be no reason for them to exist and they would lose all funding from various organizations. If they admitted that everything could be financed by creating new money, no one would ask for their advice. They prefer to enjoy a high income, saying clichés.

Then the debate over the taxes that must be levied to finance basic income is enjoyable for politicians. Politicians, of course, know much better than economists that they can simply issue government bonds to make money. They do it, anyway, all the time. They will, however, enter into the tax debate so that everyone can talk to their own political audience. The "conservative" politician will say, roughly, that he cannot tax those who work hard, for the benefit of the lazy . The 'left' will say that the rich should be taxed and the taxes should be given to the poor. None of them will clarify who is who, while for all politicians the same ceiling applies to social spending. We are seeing the end result nowadays, when the basic income for all citizens is, perhaps, more necessary than ever, has not yet been implemented, except in a few isolated cases.

The biggest problem, however, with the financing of basic income through taxation is that it tries to resolve inequality by approaching it from a completely wrong perspective. Indeed, in theory, the rich could be taxed to finance a basic income for all adult citizens It is unacceptable for policymakers to reduce the taxation of companies and the rich , when, already the central banks with QE, facilitate them. But, initially, it is difficult to implement . If the tax rate on the rich increases too much, they will declare lower incomes. The CEO, for example, of a large company will give a lower salary to himself and will look for other ways (stock options, commissions, bonuses) to make up for his lost income. At the same time, if a country imposes a high wealth tax, immediately the richest and often skilled workers needed in the country's economy will migrate to another, with a friendlier tax environment[11]. Once upon a time, only a few exotic islands, called tax havens, had almost zero taxes to attract rich people. Nowadays, even the developed countries are competing with each other to offer the lowest taxes to the rich. Recent examples are the United States, where Trump cut taxes, and France, where Macron abolished the wealth tax. So, unfortunately, the tax increase ends up burdening those who cannot hide their income, who are the poorest, cancelling the benefits of a basic income to all.

However, even if the rich pay their taxes and a basic income is set, inequality will not be addressed. The question should not be how to take the money from the rich, when the system, previously, had offered it to them so easily and without asking for anything in return. The question must be how to change the system so that it does not offer it from the beginning. The public discourse over how the rich will be taxed is completely disorienting and sounds good to politicians. There is a constant competition between the states and large companies. Usually the states has the power, while the multinationals have the money (although after the adoption of QE by the central banks and the states gained direct access to money, but in the meantime the big, especially technological, companies have gained political power). One side wants something from the other. Taxation is a tool used by politicians to blackmail the other side, earning rewards. The deal in the end, usually, is beneficial for both. It is generally a game that does not concern the ordinary people. They should not, unwittingly, take someone's side.

Finally, at this point, the rich are right. It is not their fault or at least they are not the primarily responsible for how the system is structured. When someone takes money in his hands, he considers it, rightly, his own and he will do everything to protect it . If they take it from him, he will feel wronged. It does not matter if he acquired the money through an unjust system. In this, the rich are like the poor and all people. The whole capitalist system is based on the individual's right to property. What people think is their own, they see as an extension of themselves and defend it. What needs to be done is to stop the money generated by the central banks from being channeled to the rich so that they do not subsequently acquire property rights in it.

Let's talk about the nature of money

Stop printing money?

Looking for the ideal solution to make up for the lost income due to the chronic malfunction of the labor channel, the question arises whether the printing of money should stop. If this were to happen ,money would be scarce, markets would reflect the real economy, and interest rates would be higher. In addition, loss-making companies would go bankrupt and would be replaced by other better and more innovative ones.. So far so good. Nevertheless, the predominance of a completely free market, without any intervention from the central banks, would not repair the labor channel, because it would not change the fact that man is needed less and less in the productive process. Unemployment in this case would be high, even if there was job mobility, that is, when an employee was laid off, he would be retrained immediately, if necessary, and would have no problem changing city or country to find a new job. As you can understand, a person cannot live like this, but even if he was willing to do so, he would not be sure that he would find a job with a decent salary. Maybe it would be better the money printing not to stop, but to use it better. At this point let's look how central banks create so much money that they do not lose its value. Why is there no inflation at last?

The disappearance of inflation

The generation of Millennials, let alone the younger generations have not felt and, perhaps, do not know what inflation is. Inflation occurs when the prices of goods bought by consumers increase, reducing their disposable income. It mainly affects those who are paid fixed salaries, as is usually the case with civil servants, or receive a fixed amount of money such as pension. Sometimes it has a positive effect on business profits because firms sell their products and services more expensively. In general, however, inflation is a particularly negative phenomenon, because it affects the credibility of the financial and banking system, on which the proper functioning of society depends. That is why the central banks still have as their main official goal to keep inflation low.

The main reason that there is no inflation in recent decades is the rapid development of technology. It is the technology that has upgraded the production process so much that the supply of products and services exceeds their demand. Price increases occur when a limited quantity of goods is placed on the market in relationship with consumer demand. In this case the price of these goods goes up so much as to exclude the consumers who want to buy them but do not have the money or are not willing to pay more than a certain price. The final price is formed at the point where the requested quantity is equal to the offered one. A typical example of a market where demand is greater than supply is the urban housing market. In this case, many people want to rent or buy limited number of homes. The end result is an increase in rents and property prices. The high cost of housing in big cities is one of the most important problems in the modern world. These high costs, in fact, are not reflected, usually, in the official inflation indicators, which include other basic goods. Fortunately, the previous case is the exception to the rule. The rule is that industry can produce more goods than humanity can consume, something is not expected to change in the future. That is why the prices of products do not increase, which would reduce the value of money. There is, however, something more that makes the money of the modern age different from the money of the John Law era

Money as a reminder of our common destiny

It is said that people in modern times do not trust the institutions[1]. They do not trust the government, the justice, the media, etc. The cost of mistrust is insecurity and lack of meaning. All of the above are true, but at the same time, it crosses one's mind that there must be something that unites people, something that makes possible the basic functioning of society. This, as common and trivial as it may sound, is money. People do not pay attention to it, because they take its value for granted. They forget that, like other institutions, this is also a human creation. It is the earthly god that humans have created to believe, without a doubt. Money is a value, visible and earthly and not in the realm of imagination. It transcends the ethnic, racial, religious, political differences of the people and with this perspective unites them all.

Even more striking is that people's faith in money is not shaken, even if the central banks print it in these huge quantities every day. This begs the question: if something increases in quantity, does its value decrease accordingly? Economists have thus taught the world to think. Economics is the science of rarity. They have adopted this way of thinking because natural resources are limited and people are competing for them. Thus, what is not available in large quantities is more valuable than what is in abundance.

The mistake was that the economists carried the same approach, which forbids, what is in abundance, to have much value, and in the valuation of money. That is why most people take it for granted that when money is printed in such large quantities it will become inflationary and when it does not, they say it will become so in the future. Inflation means that the price / value of money falls. This is not the case, because the people of this planet have created these currencies and trust them no matter what happens. They have nothing else to trust. The mindset , however, of economists takes the form of an axiom, from which it is difficult for one to escape, and so occasionally, perhaps, people experience a kind of cognitive dissonance. When, for example, someone is told that the ECB prints euros every day, subconsciously, perhaps, he thinks that this is negative for the euro, which is nothing more than a piece of paper, but the next moment he may use the same useless piece of paper for shopping. The necessary condition, of course, for this to happen is that there an abundance of goods. If there is nothing to buy to eat, have fun, etc., no money in the world has any value. Even if someone had gold , which is considered the most precious metal and currency once, would it be useless if there was no food? Fortunately, advances in technology make it possible to produce goods in greater quantities than humanity can consume.

The same outdated way of thinking of economists is adopted by the followers of bitcoin and cryptocurrencies in general. They are presented as alternatives to national currencies, arguing that they are more valuable because they can only be created in limited quantities as opposed to conventional ones. If cryptocurrencies ever replace conventional ones, it will not be because they will be available in limited quantities, but because people will trust them more. Until then, they will be suitable for speculation in order for their holders, eventually convert them into US dollars or euros and become rich. The fact that their value increases compared to conventional currencies is due to the market bubble, which the central banks created. In addition, the fact that they cannot be printed, from one point onwards, like conventional currencies is a negative feature. The predominance of cryptocurrencies will mean the stabilization of social class differences. The lords of the world, in this case, will be the first to mine cryptocurrencies with their computing power. As in the beginning of human history, kings were the ones who occupied the gold mines.

Ultimately, the belief in money, combined with the abundance of goods, is what separates the John Law era from the modern. John Law printed French pounds, but no one trusted them. The big central banks are doing the same now, but in modern times everyone trusts the US Fed dollars ,the ECB euro and so on. The other important development is that gradually not only the currencies of developed economies are being trusted, but also those of developing ones.

The trust scale of national currencies

People have always wanted to be able to measure their wealth. Money was the right tool not only to measure the value of their property, but also to store it. In modern times, anything one owns has a value measured in euro, US dollars, etc. and feels safe knowing that he can convert it, if needed, into banknotes of the above currencies. The adoption of today's national currencies, which everyone knows and trusts, did not happen overnight, but gradually, as globalization progressed.

In the past, when the convertibility of national currencies into gold was in force, in times of crisis everyone converted their banknotes into it. Gold was considered to have the maximum value and was used to replace their banknotes and other assets, if necessary. In 1971 the convertibility of national currencies into gold was permanently abolished and people were left with only them[2]. Even though national currencies have no intrinsic value, like gold, but are made of cheap materials, people accepted them. Everyone agreed that they had value. They had no other choice. Something has value when it is accepted by everyone, such as the euro and the US dollar. With the interconnection of all the inhabitants of the planet, the agreement became global.

When the convertibility of currencies into gold was abolished, the next distinction as to what has value was made in the context of national currencies. It was considered that the safest currencies are those of the great powers, which dominate the geopolitical field. Each national currency holds a place in a imaginary 'trust scale' in the consciousness of people. At the top of the world's 'trust scale' was and is the US dollar. It is the currency in which oil, metals, natural gas, etc. are priced. With this, more than 60% of world trade is made[3]. In general, the 'national currency trust scale' is divided into two parts . On the one hand are the safe currencies of developed economies and on the other the less reliable currencies of emerging economies.

The last few decades have been full of incidents in which investors sell large quantities of a developing country's currency to buy a safer one. The sequence of events includes acceleration of the sell-off, hyperinflation and poverty of the country where the currency is devalued. The official excuse, when these incidents occur, is that the country was fiscally irresponsible and markets punished it. Eventually the affected country is unable to meet its debt obligations.

Somewhere there the IMF intervenes, lending it in a reliable currency, usually US dollars, in exchange for reforms and cuts in public spending. Liberal reforms make sense, because if an economy becomes freer, money moves more easily and economic activity can recover faster. But as logical as imposing of economic reforms is, the imposing of austerity is just as absurd. The official explanation, always, is that in this way the country will restore its credibility to investors. The results are always the same. The economy stagnates. Reforms that would normally be positive, are not being implemented, because those who benefit from their non-abolition, in the face of the poverty spectrum, react strongly. The sell-off of government bonds and the currency is accelerating even more and poverty is rising.

The austerity imposed by the IMF is purely punitive and has no economic logic. Those who claim that, if a country cuts its government spending, the markets will reward it, are nonsense. The credibility of national economies does not increase when countries spend recklessly, but by no means does it increase when they stop altogether. An economy in which money does not circulate, due to the austerity applied, is not attractive to anyone.

The credibility of an economy depends primarily, not on the country's fiscal data, but on how people perceive its economy. Ultimately from the position of its currency in the 'trust scale'. For example, no one can imagine the bankruptcy of the United States, which has the largest arsenal in the world. If it depended on how high a country's debt was, one would expect emerging economies to be full of debt and developed economies to have few. In fact, as the chart below shows, the opposite is true. Since the 1990s, the debts of developed countries have been growing steadily more than those of developing countries. Many times, when the great powers made recommendations to other countries for their high deficits and debts, they themselves were in a worse fiscal position. They abused their advantage due to the fact that their national currencies occupied higher positions in the "trust scale" of world currencies. Thus, not only did they borrow more money, but also at lower interest rates. This does not mean that emerging economies, whose currency was depreciating at record pace and their government bonds were not accepted, did not have high deficits, but that their fiscal position had a complementary effect on the low level of confidence that their national currency had.

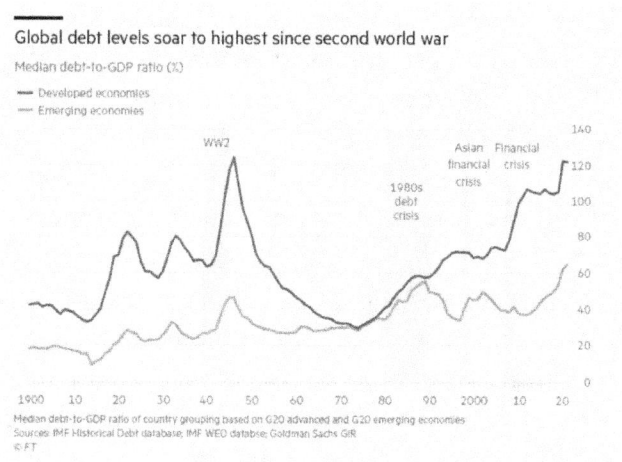

Global debt levels soar to highest since second world war
Median debt-to-GDP ratio (%)
— Developed economies
— Emerging economies
Median debt-to-GDP ratio of country grouping based on G20 advanced and G20 emerging economies
Sources: IMF Historical Debt database; IMF WEO database; Goldman Sachs GIR
© FT

The critical point, shown in the chart above, was in 2008. At that time, there was a sharp increase in the debt of developed economies compared to that of emerging economies. 'Coincidentally', then the central banks of developed countries began to print money. The first central bank to adopt QE was the Fed, which can create the most reliable currency on the planet. The United States took full advantage of the dominance of the US dollar in the ' trust scale" of currencies to fund the US government. If the central banks of the developing economies did this, the result would be that their currencies would depreciate, but because the central banks of the developed economies did, there were no serious consequences. There was, however, one that appeared in 2020.

The national currencies of developed economies may not have lost their lead in the 'trust scale' of national currencies, but at the same time the national currencies of emerging economies have risen. The result was that in 2020, for the first time in history, the central banks of emerging economies began to buy their countries' government bonds, that is, to print their own currency.[4] Investors are gradually realizing that they can protect the value of their assets converting them into currencies other than those of developed economies. Why , for example, the US dollar is the best , when it is printed at a higher pace than any other currency on the planet? Maybe it is not. The gradual equality between national currencies paves the way for all the world's central banks to be able to print their currency without a limit. And if they can, they will. Free money is gradually spreading around the globe.

Central banks have another reason to print their national currency in addition to financing their public sector . By printing a country its currency, it can devalue it against other national currencies, which is a good thing. No country wants to have a overvalued currency, which hurts its exports. So there is a chance we will face the strange spectacle that each country will compete with the others for who will print more money. Imagine the amount of money that will flood the financial markets and how many powerful people and dictators will emerge from this process, if it continues.

Before we move on, we cannot ignore the fact that the gradual increase in the reliability of the currencies of developing countries has, also, a positive side. At some point, the separation of economies as developed and developing must be a thing of the past. Maybe at some point the powerful countries will lose their ability to intervene in other countries' economies, because the latter will not need them for loans. Emerging economies will be able to be financed by their central banks. The dark side to this positive development is that the freedom that one country will enjoy in its relations with others may not translate into the freedom of its citizens if a dictator , who can make money out of thin , takes power.

The new money channel

Central banks can create money in huge quantities without losing its value for two reasons: technology, and our faith in money. Technology is the one that replaces people in production, reducing the available jobs, but technology is also the one that reduces the general price level and therefore increases the value of money. What takes away from us, returns to us much more. It is not technology's fault that we have allowed its gift to be managed by some rich and powerful people who serve only their own interests . As far as our belief in a specific set of national currencies , this is also a collective achievement. This has happened gradually over the centuries, when we realized that there is no one else to save us, but we are alone on this planet and we have to define what has value. We have decided that value is included in some specific currencies that are not gold or silver and with this agreement we move forward. Two collective achievements of humanity and not of the central banks. We trust the money and not the central banks that produce it. The central banks are taking advantage of our confidence in money. Developments have long outpaced central banks. Their traditional economic policy tools are outdated. They just hide their incompetence behind incomprehensible words.

The money printed by the central banks should go directly to us . It would be, also, the most right policy with economic criteria. The disposable income of us would increase. Hence, our consumption as well, and therefore business profits . The money would go to people who, for the most part, would spend it and not put it on the stock market. If this were to happen, the money that central banks would need to print would be much less than what they print nowadays, and the economic growth would be much higher.

In any case, the supposedly ultimate goal of central bank interventions since 2008 is for money to reach us. It just has to go through the markets first, reach the companies and the states and finally us. We do not mention the banks, because, as we said, they play a minimal role in this network. It makes sense, making the money so many stops, too little to reach its final destination. It is forbidden to bypass and reach people directly. It must pass through the markets in order to be fairly distributed to the considered pillars of the system.. Then, the companies, supposedly, will decide with purely technocratic and therefore objective criteria how much of the money they will redirect to the labor channel and how much for investment. While the government of each country, acting according with the interests of its citizens, who elected it, will proceed with social spending and public investment. As we explained, of course, the real result is that most of the money, trapped in the stops, makes the rich richer and the strong stronger. We are not considered worthy to manage the money. Others will always decide for us, with their fair and infallible criteria, and always for our good. All the officials of the political-economic system claim that nothing else can be done.

Indeed, if we accept that this money distribution network cannot be changed, nothing else can be done. The only thing that can be done is what the central banks did in 2020, when they printed even more money. Since a small percentage of the money goes to us , the only way to get more money is for the central banks to channel even more into the money distribution network. The result is that a little more money reaches us and a lot more money to those people who have already benefited from the system. What a convenient solution for all the powerful on the planet , my God! What a coincidence that no one is thinking of installing another channel through which the money of the central banks will be channeled directly to us !

Although this is not, absolutely true. They have also considered sending us money directly. They called it 'helicopter money' [5], but they consider it so extreme that it has been on the agenda since the 1960s. They think it is less extreme for central banks to buy , from the money they created out of thin air, almost all the government bonds issued in 2020 and to skyrocket stock market indices in a year of deep recession. We do not know what worse must happen to humanity than the coronavirus pandemic, to judge that they can send a fraction of the money they print now, to the citizens of this planet. It is obvious that nothing will change if we sit idly by, waiting for the agents of the system to act. They will continue to pretend to be fools, as long as it goes. In any case, the new channel must be permanent and not occasional.

A new permanent channel of money must be created, which will supplement and replace, if necessary, the labor channel. Each of us must enjoy a basic income, unconditionally, financed by the printed money of the central banks. More goods and better goods are being produced than at any other time in human history in this world, but many people do not have the money to buy them because the money distribution network has not changed. A working person can no longer make a living most of the time. Continuing to channel large sums of money through the existing network will make things worse every time, causing inequalities and over-increasing the power of states and multinationals.

It is time for the economic survival of every citizen to stop being a field of political controversy. If the available goods were in limited quantities, it would make sense for a "wise" state to intervene to distribute them fairly and to implement policies to increase them. In the modern world, where there is free trade between countries, this is not the case. There is an overabundance of goods, which has given birth to an overabundance of money. All the state had to do was transfer the free money to us and, after having done so, implement other economic policies. Unfortunately, while it sounds simple, it's made so that it cannot. We all know better than anyone else what is best for us. All we needs is money to be able to live with dignity and be able to determine the course of our life without stress. This should have been our basic right for a long time.

As far as multinationals are concerned, there have been recent discussions about their social responsibility and whether they can also help humanity[6]. It is understandable that in order to reach the young people who are their most dynamic clientele, they adopt political positions and attitudes, which express them more. They do it to sell more and to have a bigger role in politics. It is understandable and acceptable. Beyond that, it is a pity that there are people who seriously claim that the goal of large companies today is the overall well-being of society. We do not want other saviors. We want the obvious, without being obligated to anyone.

The third pillar

The consumer unions

But let us be realistic, politicians would never allow the economy to detach so much from politics. If no one's economic situation depends on the economic policies of the state, politicians will lose much of their power. To maintain the status quo they would use all their communication tricks, which have become experts in recent years and if they used only propaganda, we would be lucky. How much more so if we consider that we live in an environment in which the conditions are perfect for politicians to gain more and more power and, as is well known, power is addictive. As the years go by, it will become more difficult for everyone to find a well-paying job. Politicians of all spectrums will then intervene and 'save' us. Inevitably, at some point a basic income for everyone will become an official policy.

Most likely, the Millennials generation will not experience it, but it will happen when unemployment reaches such high levels and workers' incomes fall so much that a social unrest would be very likely. It will, however, be a basic income so low that the people will barely survive, while, at the same time, it will be said that the money came from taxation and not from the freshly printed money of the central banks. Again it will be said that the debts will be repaid. The hypocrisy that we are experiencing today will not change at all. The new measure will also be accepted by politicians who support the orthodox economic thinking. It is already the current trend the center-right politicians to adopt traditional social-democratic economic measures while supporting low debt and zero deficits.

Thus, in the current context, the pressure for political change will hardly lead to a definitive solution to the economic problem. The only definitive solution would be for the people to have direct access to central banks money and this never seems likely to happen. Let us consider, at this point, what is the network through which the free money of the central banks is distributed in the two pillars of the system. As we have said, this is done through financial markets. So, the only way for people to have direct access to free money would be if they also had access to the financial markets. That is, if, in a way, they also issued bonds.

In order for an institution to be able to issue bonds it must have a source of income. States have revenue from taxes and businesses from their sales. But do we have something that someone would be willing to buy? The answer is yes. We must not forget that each of us is a consumer at the same time. We must not forget this nature of ours . Companies, which want to sell their products, pay money to advertising companies to entice us. That is, they give money to others to attract our consumer power. But why give them to others and not to us ? Is such a thing possible? Before we answer we will take a quick look at what is happening in the field of advertising.

Now, the amount spent annually on advertising by companies worldwide is about $ 600 billion[1], of which, more than half, goes to online advertising. The usual process was and still is, to a large extent, companies placing their ads in newspapers, in public events, in prominent places on the road network, etc. Generally, in places where we are more likely to notice them. Then, if we look at them, it is possible to be interested and finally buy some of the advertised products. Essentially, those who promote their products in this way, spend their money blindly.

Advertising changed with the connection of all the people of the world through the internet. A new place appeared, which is the internet, where almost all the consumers of the world gathered every day. In this way, those who wanted to advertise found the most visible spot in the world to distract us. Again, though, most ads continue to go unnoticed by internet users . The big breakthrough came when some companies started monitoring our behaviour on the internet so that they could promote ads for products that suit our tastes. In fact, these companies, which are mainly Facebook, Amazon and Google, have so much power, economic and political, because they can, to a large extent, control our consumer power. It is said that our personal data is the new gold. But is that so? The gold has always been and is our consuming power. Simply, by utilizing our personal data, the specific technology companies were able to control our power. So if we found a way to direct it where we wanted , we would limit the power of the big technology companies and , most importantly, we would earn money.

The way to direct our consumer power is to define a specific place in which we will do our shopping. Now this is possible because we do not need to walk physical distances to do our shopping. We can also make them online from home. All we have to do is to set up a consumer union, which will create a site, where companies can exhibit their products and in which, each of us will have a personal account. Basically, to create a marketplace like Amazon. At the same time, we are committed to making our online purchases only from this site. In this way we will all unite our consumer power so that we can negotiate it. Then we would tell the firms, that if they wanted us to buy their goods online, they had to pay us in order to show them in our digital market. If this were to happen, companies would pay too much for their products to be in the only place on the internet where they could sell their products online. Their ads on our site would be much more likely to turn into sales than those that exist today, because they would be located in the most visible space of the internet and would be our only choices in our online shopping. We as consumers would not sacrifice anything. Our consumer choices would not be limited. We would spend our money on the same products because, again, the same companies would give their money to promote them. What would change would be that for the first time in history advertising revenue would not go to Silicon Valley companies, but to our pockets. The icing on the cake would be that these companies would lose much of their influence in our lives. Maybe, they defined less what we read, what we buy, how we have fun, etc.

Here one would say: it would be nice for companies to pay us to buy their products, but, let's be little realistic, the money raised could not be enough for all of us . First of all, it would not be little. Let's take a look at the numbers. Suppose a global consumer union was created, which set up a site like Amazon , in which we would do all our shopping.

Wouldn't this site earn at least ¼ of the global advertising revenue ? If that happened , with the current data, approximately would be about $ 150 billion. This means that since the world population is about 7.5 billion, if the amount was evenly distributed, each inhabitant of the Earth would receive $ 20. It is not a small amount of money, if we take into account that minors and residents of countries with very low GDP would receive it. The main point, however, is another. In the previous hypothetical case of the creation of a global consumer union, $ 150 billions would not be distributed to people, but would be used as a guarantee for the issuance of bonds. Let' s call them consumer bonds.

Do not forget we live in the age of free money. The aim of the consumer union would be to cover, at least, the interest of a one-year consumer bond . Even if the bond yield, issued by the world consumer union, was 2%, the $ 150 billion would cover interest on an annual bond of $ 7.5 trillion. That is, $ 1,000 for each person of the Earth for one year. A decent amount, having assumed that the interest rate will be 2%, at a time when in 2020, of the bonds issued worldwide, only about 15% of them had a higher yield.

In the current environment, the bonds of such an organization, with such a stable source of income, would be in high demand and would have an interest rate much lower than 2%. Investors would buy consumer bonds not out of charity, but because they would like to make more money. The central banks would not even have to buy them by printing money. Nowadays private investors buy bonds of zombie companies, which cannot even cover the interest on their bonds. Would not they buy the consumer bonds?

It is the only way, the favorable environment created by the central banks for issuing of bonds, to be used for something positive. In this world, anyone who does not have access to the free money is lost. Only if we all unite our consumer power behind a single entity could we gain access to it. The consumer unions that would be created could be organized at the level of countries or associations of countries. They could even be thematic, ie set up based on the type of products that will be sold on their digital platform. As for the platform, it could offer ads to any user, depending on their shopping history. What we need to do is to take the initiative . The practical issues will be resolved.

There are two other critical issues that need to be addressed. The first is in what form the money of a consumer union would be distributed. The amount raised by the consumer bonds would be better distributed to us in the form of consumer vouchers rather than cash. Even if the previous action would limit our freedom a little, it is considered necessary for any consumer union to have high revenue. Companies would give us more money if they knew there was a good chance they would be refunded multiple times through our online shopping. In any case, if someone did not want to spend money on shopping, it would mean that they did not need it.

The second is how the money of consumer union would be distributed. In order for such a consumer union to function smoothly and not turn into a bureaucratic monster, like the state apparatus and multinational corporations, it would have to operate, with specific, clear and transparent rules. The simplicity of its operation would be ensured if the same amount of money was distributed to all adult citizens. This distribution may had been unfair, because some people would get money they did not need, but it would be better than creating corruption and bureaucracy within the consumer union. If the money was distributed, only to those who needed it most, which would be fairer, a large group would have to be appointed to determine who they were. In such a case, everyone would be motivated to hide their income and bribe the team, which would determine the beneficiaries of the consumer voucher. The end result would be the creation of a second state. At the same time, the whole process of identifying beneficiaries would divide people. Those who did not receive the aid would suspect those who did. The main goal of any consumer union should be for each of its members to be able to buy the products they need so that they can live comfortably, regardless of what others do. So from the moment someone became a member of a consumer union they would automatically have the right to receive consumer vouchers.

The proposed solution has an additional positive feature. It is in line with the mindset of QE. Let us remember its definition. According to the Bank of England, the ultimate goal of QE 'is to boost consumption and investment in the economy'. The emphasis is always on investment because, in theory, they result in long-term economic growth. That is, they do not only increase the consumption of an economy in the period in which they occur, but they also create the conditions for an increase in consumption in the future. Unfortunately, as we have said, this is not because investment does not necessarily create new jobs. This is why their contribution to a country's economic activity is usually only short-term.

They try to increase short-term consumption, mainly in two ways: by making the rich richer and by giving money to states to proceed with targeted social spending. Unfortunately, the rich already have so much money that they cannot spend much more, while states are unable to increase their spending to the size that society needs. In theory, central banks are promoting consumption growth in a third way. Having set interest rates so low, each of us has a greater incentive to get a loan from a bank, because we will have to pay less interest. These loans, however, have a problem. They are personal and must be repaid in a relatively short time. Unfortunately there is not an intangible and immortal organization such as states and companies to take the loans instead of us. So the increase in consumption, and in the third way, cannot be significant.

If consumer unions were created, however, it would be possible for them to borrow instead of us. At the same time, central banks would find a new way to stimulate consumption, without having to do anything different than today. They would continue to support the market , ensuring favorable financing conditions in the two existing pillars of the system, which issue bonds. The only thing that would change would be that in this case there would be an additional body that would issue bonds, which would be the consumer unions. In essence, a new third pillar would be created, from which money would flow . A third pillar, which would not only provide us with a comfortable living, but also make it easier for central banks to directly stimulate economic activity.

In the current environment, the privileged are, of course, the managers of states and large corporations. With the excuse that they are doing something important they control the flow of money. It is obvious that this is unfair. The well-being of every person is as noble a goal as that of states and multinationals. Relying, however, on what is fair and what makes sense, unfortunately, can have little effect on the present. What always makes the difference is who has the power and we as consumers have it. Some consider it a good idea to revive trade unions. They are wrong. We cannot put pressure on companies as employees, since we are not so necessary to them. If we overplay our hand they will replace us with robots and new production systems. The above will happen anyway at some point. The only power we have is as consumers. If we unite our power we can achieve a lot. Now, it is possible to do that. At a time when more and more consumers are shopping online, it is our chance to create consumer unions , instead of mourning the jobs lost in retail.

Consumer unions , which will issue consumer bonds can be made. Since companies would be willing to give us money to list their products in our exclusive online marketplace and investors would buy our consumer bonds, any further discussion is unnecessary. No state can stop us. All we have to do is agree that all our online shopping will be done by a specific website, which we will have set up before. It will not be so difficult, considering that, if we succeeded, most of this shopping would be done with free money.

Inflation again

The main fear is what will happen next. What disaster would strike the world? The answer is that nothing negative would happen, on the contrary, people would have more money, feel safer and enjoy more goods. It takes a lot of brainwashing for a positive event to be treated with so much suspicion. If everyone was asked, personally, how they would feel, if they had more money to spend, it would be difficult for someone to answer not good. It is absurd to say that if this happened to everyone at the same time, it would be catastrophic.

We know what the experts will say and most will agree. They will say that inflation will come and money will lose its value. It does not matter that the central banks print trillions dollars, euro etc in recent years and inflation is nowhere to be seen. They will say the same thing again. They will say that evil will happen in the future and that is why people must be protected now. But again, what has been said before about the reasons that we do not have inflation, would apply even then. There is no inflation, because the production of goods exceeds demand. If people increased their consumption, the prices would not rise, because the production process has improved so much that it would meet the increased demand. In any case, global demand has a ceiling that is determined by the finite needs of a consumer and the number of consumers. At a time when the world population is shrinking, this ceiling is also lowering, so the increase in demand would be limited. Even the prices and rents of real estate in the cities would fall, because people would no longer have to concentrate on them, to find work. These, easily understood by all, are distorted by economists.

When the United States in early 2021 passed a $ 1.9 trillion fiscal package through the Senate, most economists argued that such a large package would cause inflation[2]. They said that US citizens would increase their consumption so much that US production, and in some sectors, global production would not be able to meet it. The immediate result would be companies to increase their salaries in order to attract new employees. Until now, they said, companies did not have to do this because there were available workers who were either unemployed or not looking for work. But by giving so much money to American consumers, the US economy would approach its full potential. So companies would be forced to pay higher wages to lure more people to work for them , including those who until then did not want, for their own reasons, to work. An increase in wages would translate to an increase in production costs, which would lead to an increase in prices. In addition, they claimed that the first wave of inflation would be followed by a second, when the US economy would finally overheat making full use of its resources. Then the produced goods would be not enough for the American consumers, resulting in an increase in their prices. Economists did not say this narrative exactly like that, but quoting a lot of economic terminology, so that no one understood anything. Essentially though, this was said, which while it seems logical, is nonsense.

The narrative that the volume of production depends on the number of workers comes from another era, which is long gone. Industrial production takes place, as we have seen, with an ever-decreasing human presence. The processing and modification of the raw materials in the final product is carried out, almost exclusively, by advanced machines. At this point one might say that labor costs may not increase, but the cost of raw materials and energy will, if production volume increases too much. But here, too, technology has done its miracle. Every year it is possible to produce more goods using fewer and cheaper raw materials.[3] There are many examples. Renewable energy is gradually replacing fossil fuel energy production, which is not only positive for the environment, but also reduces overall energy costs. New crops require less water etc. The end result of all these technological developments is that modern industrial products have a production cost so small that it is covered by 10-15% of their price[4]. That's why companies spend $ 600 billion a year on advertising and have created so many unprofitable bureaucratic jobs. They make so many profits that they do not know how to spend it. And then the central banks come and give them extra free money. After what has been said, how likely do you think the scenario is that wages will increase excessively and production will not be able to meet the increased demand ?

Economists make noise because they are losing their jobs and over time on they will make more and more noise . Technology, like many other categories of workers, makes them obsolete. In the age of abundance, the science of economics has no place, except in specific and limited areas of the general economics. Their grand narratives refer to times of the past. Once upon a time they were the stars, now they cannot be. They must accept it. The Biden administration, because of the situation (not only because of the pandemic, but also because the Democrats won a majority in the Senate, so they could pass some bills without the Republican vote), increased social spending more than usual. So instead of applauding its attitude, they criticized it . They did not mention to the achievement that occurred during the pandemic. Think, in such adverse conditions, in which world production was under-functioning and the transport of goods, due to lockdowns, was difficult, for a whole year, there were only minimal price increases and shortages of products. They preferred to occupy the public sphere referring to the unlikely scenario in which world production would not be able to meet the increased demand after the pandemic. Even if this happens, it will be a temporary phenomenon, which will last until the production process adapts to the new conditions. Imagine their reaction if what is suggested in this book is ever adopted .

The only possible increase could be in the payment of jobs, which are still done exclusively by people. From the ever-shrinking number of these professions, two stand out: caring for infants and the elderly. But it's fine. It would be a positive fact that the above jobs would finally gain the recognition and pay they deserve. Now most avoid these jobs, considering them inferior, while they are so important for the well-being of people. At least much more important than most high-paying managerial and financial jobs.

The paradox is that inflation is more likely to occur at some point if the current conditions, which are typical of the free money era, remain, and not if the money was given directly to the people. This can happen in three ways. Initially, the easy financing of companies has the effect of thriving two types of them. On the one hand are the big companies that buy potential competitors before they grow and on the other the zombie companies that just survive. Both types lead to monopoly or oligopoly situations. When in a sector there is one company that acquires the others, it essentially establish a monopoly. Similarly few companies establish an oligopoly, when they acquire the others. However, there is also an oligopolistic environment, even if an industry is dominated by zombie companies. This is because new companies cannot enter the industry, because the existing zombie companies earn all the revenue. Monopoly or oligopoly conditions in a market can lead to a price increases. This can happen when companies in an industry, because they are not afraid to lose market share, neglect their production.

In such a case, they may not be able to meet the demand for their products and thus be forced to increase their prices. In addition, it is possible for inflation to increase for reasons not related to the production process, but to the speculation of companies, because, having no competition to face, there is no one to prevent them from raising the prices of their products. It is impressive that today, despite the existence of monopolies and oligopolies, no price increases are observed. It is another indication of how much technology has reduced production costs and has increased the profit margins so that corporate mismanagement and speculation do not translate into price increases. Nevertheless, it would be good to restore free competition between companies.

Another phenomenon that is due to the action of central banks and can lead to inflation, is the irrational rise of financial markets. Most people feel that the stock market does not concern them. As we have explained, of course, markets today are the main way in which inequality increases, making the rich richer. Nevertheless, one could argue that since it does not affect our daily lives, we can let them rise. Unfortunately, again, things are more complicated. If the same situation continues, soon, we will all experience negative consequences in our daily lives. The hunt for investors for ever-increasing returns is very likely to lead to a large increase in the price of all commodities (oil, copper, silver, etc) traded in the markets. This trend has already started to appear at the end of 2020. It seems like the natural continuation of the bubble, which does not break, of the stock markets. After all, the right to own a quantity of, say, copper, is more valuable than a share of a loss-making company .At least copper, the investors know it has some value. It is a metal that can be seen and touched . If this happens, the rise in prices of the products we consume will hardly be avoided. It is somewhat ironic that inflation may ultimately arise not from the increase in demand for raw materials used in production, but from the increase in demand for their financial derivatives. It is possible that prices will not rise due to increased consumer demand , but only for some investors to gain a few percentage points higher return.

The anxiety of the rich to find a place to invest their money, leads us to the third way in which there can be excessive price increases. This time, however, not in general, but specifically in house prices. Real estate prices in urban centers are already high due to their limited supply. However, their prices are rising even more, because super- rich people do not know where to put their money. As we said, they put them mainly on financial markets, but many times that is not enough. There are no researches that determine the rate of increase in property prices due to the forces of supply and demand and that due to the speculation of the rich. Nevertheless, everyone's daily experience offers many examples of luxury homes in which buyers do not live. What is even more absurd is that many times these properties remain uninhabited without offering any income to their owners other than expenses. They buy them just because they feel insecure about having their money in the form of cash, even if it is enough to live many lives . Thus, in order for the rich to fight their insecurity due to their excessive wealth, they cause financial insecurity to everyone else. It is a situation that can become uncontrollable. It is no coincidence that real estate prices, as soon as the pandemic began to recede and after the central banks had printed so much money making the rich richer, soared internationally.[5] This time the increase was not limited to urban centers, but was general. It is another sign that the policy of Quantitative Easing, after its excessive use when coronavirus appeared, no longer has positive consequences for society as a whole anymore.

If there is inflation due to the conditions created by central banks in the financial markets, the consequences can be catastrophic. Economists immediately will show up and say 'we told you so', even if the price increase is not be due to real market conditions. The central banks, not having a ready-made manual to operate in the age of free money, will return to their outdated old manual, stopping printing of money and raising interest rates. This will translate into bankruptcy of many companies and hence unemployment and poverty. In such a case, as paradoxical as it sounds, the only hope will be politicians, who in order to avoid the consequent social unrest, will ignore the 'experts.' The only job of economists anyway, now, is to be used by politicians to justify their economic measures, but only if, at the same time, they are in line with their political plans. When "experts" advise them to apply excessive austerity, which none of their voters will want, it is very likely that politicians will not apply it. None of the above will happen if the central banks redirect free money from financial markets directly to people.

The end of the third pillar as the beginning of a new era

The issuance of consumer bonds by the third pillar would be a transitional stage in the ideal scenario. It would be the stage at which the pillar of the people would become institutional , taking advantage of the environment created by the central banks in the markets. It would not adequately address extreme inequality, as the most money would continue to flow into states and companies, but, at the very least, would provide a permanent income to ordinary people. In addition, the people would have their institution to push for wider change.

In an ideal world, the money generated by central banks would go directly to the people alone. Everyone will have recognized the problem and the third pillar will be unnecessary. Every citizen of the world will have a basic income financed by the free money of the central banks. The new money, this time, will be transferred from the people to the other two pillars and not the other way around, which is happening now. People will spend the free money, resulting in an increased economic activity. Thus the profits of companies will be increased, as well as the tax revenues of the states. This means that the existing two pillars will continue to have sufficient funding. Simply, what will be different will be that this time people will control the flow of money. From this perspective, it seems absurd what is happening now that there is a reverse flow.

Central banks interventions in the financial markets will stop. The prices of bonds, stocks and various financial derivatives will be determined by the real economy and not by the speculation of the rich. The indirect or direct funding of the states and the large corporations by central banks will cease. In this way, the extreme inequality that exists today will be addressed. This does not mean that inequality will disappear completely, but it will be significantly reduced. In addition to eradicating poverty, there will be a greater correlation between wealth and social contribution. Not like now, if one has a privileged position in the system, one also has access to lot of money. The free money will be distributed equally to people . Beyond that, whoever wants more, should try harder to get it. At the same time, businesses and states will function much better.

Businesses will compete with each other globally to produce the best goods. They will not be divided into those that can issue bonds and the small and medium-sized ones that cannot. The competition between them will prevent once and for all the scenario of price increases at some point. There will be no reason to save companies that do not survive the competition. Nowadays, they are saved, so that there would be no redundancies or because they are considered systemic. In a world where people have money, it will not be necessary. The bankruptcy of the companies will be due to the fact that they did not produce goods that consumers preferred and not because they did not have the money to buy them. Instead, companies that enjoy consumer preference, will have high profits and therefore money to invest without the need for additional support from central banks. The capitalism will work for the benefit of humanity, not because it is inherently good, but because it will not need man in the productive process.

In a world where politicians have less power and people have money, everything will be better. Citizens will no longer see the state as a means of livelihood and will demand responsibility and good services from it. Therefore, politicians should be more responsible. In our time detailed financial planning is not required on their part. If the government money is depleted, they can issue government bonds to raise additional revenue. In a world where this would not be so easy, they will have to submit detailed and cost- effective financial plans. If they do not fulfill their promises they will have no excuse. In a country where its citizens have money, the tax revenue will be enough for the state to provide adequate services in education, defense and health. Government revenues will come from the taxation of economic activity, which will be increased due to higher consumption. Of course, the income that every citizen receives from the central banks will not be taxed. There will also be money so that the state can finance any infrastructure projects that its citizens want. Finally, it will be able to implement, more effectively, economic policies that favor investment in environmentally friendly technologies, but at the same time burden the pockets of its citizens.

It is happening

In the world we live in there is a certain amount of money that more and more citizens receive every month, which is neither a salary nor a special allowance. We are talking, of course, about pensions. The usefulness and necessity of pensions is not in question. Everyone has to have some money in the last period of their life, during which they cannot work. The question is where does this money come from. The conventional answer is that it is the sum of the contributions of retirees during the years they worked. But is that the case?

It is common for those who have the same profession to have set up a fund. The contributions of those who work enter the fund and the pensions of those who retire come out. All the money in the fund is invested in the markets to earn more. Few countries have retirees with individual investment accounts. Their investment is not only because for reasons of principle, but also because, especially in recent years, it is necessary so that the pension funds can meet their financial obligations.

After World War II, there were many more workers than retirees. Over the years, however, each new generation had fewer children than the previous one, until we reached our time when the trend has been completely reversed and those retiring are more than those entering the workplace. Thus the employees' contributions do not cover the pensions of those who have stopped working. There is, therefore, a deficit which need to be addressed. Most of the financial gap is covered by the returns of the pension funds.

Nowadays the financial gap is so large that the return on investment of pension funds each year must be at least 7%.[1] Its is understandable, this is a fairly large yield, which is often not achieved. The central banks, of course, are doing everything they can to help the situation by supporting the markets in case of any suspicion of a fall. There is a paradox here. The prevailing view is the exact opposite, namely is that the action of central banks is responsible for the poor state of pension funds. This view is so widespread that some German retirees have been in court for years against the ECB. In May 2020 they even achieved a judicial victory, with the result that a German court asked for more explanations from the ECB, for its QE. There is currently no risk to QE, but sets a judicial precedent. And all this while the German retirees, instead of turning against the ECB, should thank it. Like, all retirees in the world have to thank all the central banks. What happens? Traditionally, pension funds invest their cash in government bonds and cover their obligations with bond coupons. But since central banks began QE, government bond yields, as we have seen, have fallen sharply. Thus, a financial product, with which pension funds had easy profits, is no longer available in many cases. Because of this many retirees believe, that if the world's central banks did not intervene, they would enjoy higher pensions.

Their thinking is wrong in two points. First, the central banks have created an environment in which the market is almost risk-free. Without their interventions there would be many bankruptcies of companies and states. Government bonds would not be so safe if the central banks did not guarantee that they would buy them, no matter what happens. German retirees would, of course, reply that they would invest their money in German government bonds that would certainly be safe, given the strong German economy. They may be right, but all investors around the world would have the same opinion. In a financial environment where insecurity would prevail, due to the non-intervention of central banks, everyone would invest in the safest government bonds. Thus, German bonds, due to their high demand, would have a low yield. In no case would it be 7%. Perhaps in such a fluid environment, their return was either zero or negative, as it is today.

The second point they overlook is that, due to QE, such high returns on the stock market are possible, which are by no means justified by corporate profits worldwide. The previous fact, however, is not known only to us but also to pension funds managers, who act accordingly. For a few years now, they have been investing in the stock market, but also in off-assets , while abandoning the government bond market. The chart below shows, for example, that from around 2018, as the yield on 30-year US government bonds declined, pension funds gradually reduced their demand for them. Thus, the world's pension funds have adapted to the new conditions and achieve returns that would not be possible without QE.

Taking into account the above, it is understood that the intervention of central banks has a positive contribution to the sustainability of pension funds. Thanks to the central banks, the funds put their money in a market that no one loses and can have high returns on stocks, etc., which they would never achieve if they invested them in government bonds under normal conditions. The indirect contribution of central banks, however, to the survival of pension funds does not stop here. They also contribute by buying government bonds. States now contribute about 8%[2] of their revenues worldwide to support funds. A percentage that is expected to increase. One could argue, then, that there is already a kind of basic income, namely pension, which , to a large extent , is financed indirectly by the central banks.

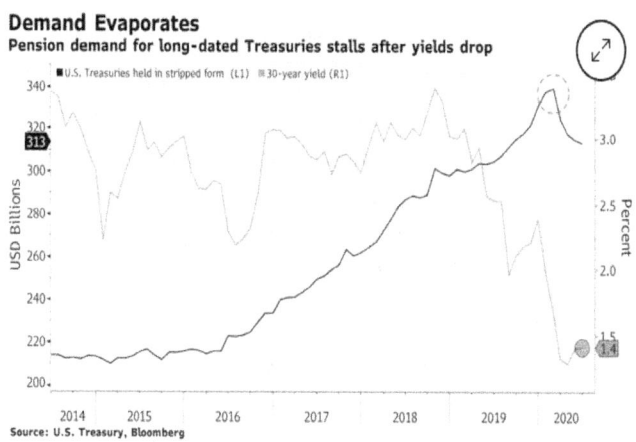

Demand Evaporates
Pension demand for long-dated Treasuries stalls after yields drop
Source: U.S. Treasury, Bloomberg

The younger ones would have no problem with the central banks printing money and channeling it, indirectly, to retirees. The point is that because they do not recognize the wider problem, real damage is being done to the lives of young people, through the gradual increase of workers' contributions. Wages, which are already low in the majority, are burdened even more by the high pension deductions. Again this hypocrisy, the officials behave as if pension system is functioning properly well and the pensions are being paid with employee contributions, which are not enough for a decent pension but are enough to make life more difficult for young people

Unfortunately, in the future, the situation will worsen. Pension funds returns should be higher and higher. Below is an estimate, made after the cooperation of reputable financial institutions, of the widening financial gap that will exist in the pension funds until 2050[3]. It seems that in 2050 the gap will reach 15.8 trillion $. How will this deficit be covered? The only way is with the new money of the central banks. Most likely it will not be fully covered. It is obvious that there is no money to pay all the pensions and the problem is global.

The only way to address pension problem radically is to be provided all adult citizens of each country with a permanent income financed by central banks. After all, in modern times, money is not enough, neither for the young, nor for the elderly. Anyone wishing to receive pension will be able to do so, but the amount of the pension will depend on actual data. That is, from the financial returns of the pensioner's contributions during the period he worked. It should be noted, however, that this time, the market will be really free and therefore investments in it will include the corresponding risk.

In any case, however, every person will be able to live without a pension, with the permanent income they will receive.

All of the above unfortunately seem impossible. Most retirees around the world are currently in the first stage of trauma, facing the harsh truth that there is not enough money for their pensions: they are in complete denial of reality. They are so desperate that they blame the central banks which, this time, by their action, help them. It is amazing how they managed, so that the dominant view to the public sphere be that the purchase of government bonds by central banks is responsible for the deficits of their pension funds. This is because today's retirees are often the most politically influential age group in the western world, and its members still hold the most key positions in power. Politicians avoid upsetting them and postponing the solution of the pension problem for later. Whenever a dilemma arises, cuts in employee benefits or cuts in pensions, the first option is always chosen. [4] But what will happen when those who are now around 30-40 years old, reach retirement age? Where will their pensions come from, when new jobs are scarce and usually low paid? What will happen when it becomes clear to everyone that the shock of the coronavirus in the service sector, which offers the majority of jobs, is not temporary? What will happen to the resulting permanent unemployed?

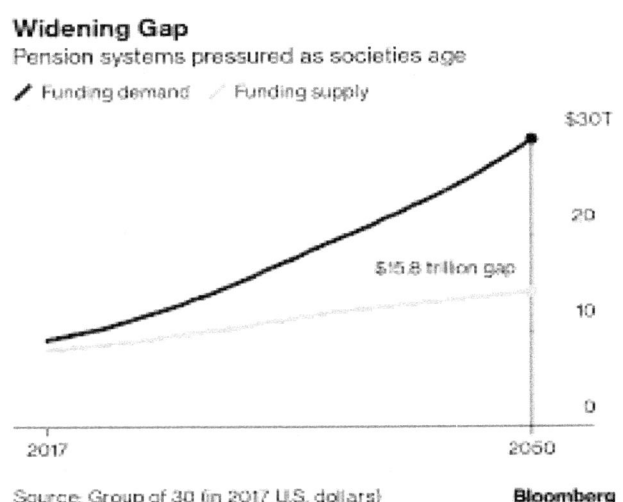

You are not your work

Jobs, from the beginning of the formation of the first cities, had as their main function the granting of identity to employees. People leaving the villages could no longer be identified by their family name. They were determined by their professional status. Work has almost never been the means of channeling human creativity and imagination. Industrialization turned most jobs into mechanical repetitions. Today, when there are not many jobs in the industry, things have not changed much. The bureaucracy, which also penetrates the private sector, has resulted in employees becoming more and more preoccupied with boring paperwork. The aforementioned category of employees is the lucky one. Most service workers are employed in jobs such as cashiers, delivery, waiters etc., in which they cannot channel their creative imagination anyway. After all, it is not surprising that only about 15% of those who work say they are happy with their job, worldwide. So while everyone wants more than anything else a successful professional career, they end up dissatisfied employees. Either they do not find the job they want, or when they find it, it is worse than they dreamed. However, for everyone, work seems like a necessary evil. Almost everyone is willing to sacrifice his creativity for the prestige and recognition that a job offers.[1]

Today, one's professional status should not be the main component of one's identity. Given that the number of new jobs that are being created is constantly decreasing and they are usually low-paid, it is against any logic to define someone from their job. This would not have happened if inequality had not arisen since the 1980s, which accelerated after 2008. The beneficiaries of the system, in order to justify their incredible wealth, told us that it was due, in addition to their special genes, to their hard work and we believed them[2].

In our time the following paradox happens: the rich work hard. In fact, they work harder than anyone else. Unlike in the 80's and earlier, when those who had more free time and had more fun were, as expected, the rich. They had more money and used it to have a good time. Now they use them to be able to work more! What happens?

What is happening is that the modern rich have lost touch with reality. Connected with the source of money that is the central banks their wealth is so unreal that it cannot be justified in any way. In their attempt to justify this, modern narcissistic rich have come to the conclusion that it is also due to the fact that they work hard. They work hard following their passion. They work hard to save the world. Their job is not a job, but their pleasure. I do not know if the above slogans remind you of anything. They come directly from the ecosystem of start-ups, in which venture capitals invest. The ecosystem that instead of producing innovation, produces slogans. The vanity bubble of Silicon Valley, created by the central banks, is made up of conceited people who congratulate each other on how special and unique they are.

Their bubble should not bother us. Everyone can be as they want and believe in what they want. The point is that they are the role models for all the people in the world. They are the best because they have the most money or vice versa. Money is traditionally used not only as a measure of one's wealth, but also for one's success. It does not matter that they became rich because of the unjust system. Since in the consciousness of the people, always, money goes hand in hand with success and recognition, the origin of money does not interest anyone. So everyone wants to become like these narcissistic beings, whose behavior is not human. Their lives, through social media, become known throughout the universe. They look flawless, happy, full of energy, committed to a high goal. They do not pretend. They are authentic. They firmly believe that they were born to save us and work tirelessly for it. The whole system promotes them. They are the elites.

We live the negative consequences of introducing some naive and unnaturally workaholic people as role models. In America in 2018, 95% of teens said that 'having a job or a career to enjoy' was very important . This was the most important priority they had in their lives. More than marriage and family, even more than making a lot of money. In the USA, the cult of work may be a little bigger than the rest of the western world, but globally, a successful professional career is still the biggest goal of young people.

It is typical that in researches on whether the provision of a basic income can work, what concerns researchers is whether those who receive it will continue to work or look for work. If it is found that those who receive money, which is not a product of labor, do not do so, the conclusion is that a basic income will have negative consequences for society. Progressives and philanthropists who want to save humanity find it unacceptable to receive free money and not work. The irony is that they are usually surprised (they are also biased that a lot of work leads to success, so it seems inconceivable that the poor can be hardworking) that the one who gets a small pocket money keeps working or looking for job[3]. It is normal, since everyone is characterized almost exclusively, sometimes, by their profession, to seek to find it, even if they have a little more money. Similarly, unfortunately, it comes as a natural consequence of workism that whoever loses his job, the mental pain they feel, most of the time, according to research, exceeds the pain caused by the death of a loved one.

What does all this mean? Nothing can change? No. If external conditions change, everything can change. If central banks stop channeling money directly to states and multinationals, the first step will have been taken. Workism will subside immediately. It will become clear to everyone that what made some people rich was not because they worked hard, but because they were the favored of an unjust system. Then, when all people receive an income, money will cease to be the main measure of success. Basically we have to let things take their natural course. Since the labor channel cannot be repaired, the officials must accept it and not try to go against the flow. The values that surround everyone's life will follow. Work will automatically cease to be the center of every human life. People will not stop working. They will simply have accepted that they may not find a job and when they do, it will probably not be permanent. Everyone fears that when a person does not have a job, he will get bored and depressed. But is that the case?

In a world where people do not necessarily have to find work to live, the lives of all of us will be much better, without a central body having to do anything. Everything will take its course. Once someone stops being defined by their job, they will find something else to be defined. People are by nature creative. In fact, modern professions suppress their creativity. It will be an opportunity to be defined , for example, by their hobbies. Let's say sculpture, painting, hiking, sewing etc. Each person will belong to one or more thematic communities, in which he / she will channel his / her creativity and receive the corresponding recognition from the other members of the community. Communities will also be online. If one is very ambitious and wants to stand out globally, there are many metric systems of success that replaces money. Let's say, the 'likes' one takes by posting on social media. Regardless of the negatives of social media, they offer an alternative to money, a measure of success. It is in our hands the age of free money to lead to a better world.

BIBLIOGRAPHY

CHAPTER 1

1. bbc.com/news/uk-politics-44524605
2. The case for people's quantitative easing. France Coppola
3. The ascent of money. Niall Ferguson
4. en.wikipedia.org/wiki/subprime_mortgage_crisis
5. A history of money from ancient times to the present day. Glyn Davies

CHAPTER 2

1. investopedia.com/ terms/ credit-easing.asp

2. reuters.com/article/us-usa-fed/bernanke-cuts-growth-view-considers-inflation-target-idUSN1845220820090218

3. lynalden.com/quantitave-easing-mmt-inflation

4. liberal.gr/technology/poses-theseis-ergasias-steroun-ta-ropot/300455

5. A world without work. Daniel Susskind

6. Work: A history of how we spend our time. James Suzman

7. lynalden.com/global-dollar-short-squeeze

8. The ascent of money. Niall Ferguson

9. 'Economic of money and banking' lecture notes from online course

   Professor Perry Mehrling, Columbia university

10. eib.org/attachements/efs/economic_report_unlocking_lending_in_europe.pdf

11. morganstanley.com/about-us-ir/earnings-releases

12. lynalden.com/quantitave-easing-mmt-inflation/

13. Good economics for hard times. Abhijit Banerjee, Esther Duflo

14. 'The wave of unicorn IPOs reveals Silicon Valley's groupthink' The economist

15. thebreadwinner/author/eric-basmajiam

16. 'Why covid-19 will make killing zombies firms off harder' The economist

17. ft.com/content/a256f8b6-11ea-a766-7c300513fe47

18. Work: A history of how we spend our time. James Suzman

19. 'The new servant class' Derek Thompson, The atlantic

20. oecd.org/gov/government-at-a-glance-2017-highlights-en.pdf

21. investopedia.com/ask/aswers/052815/does-raising-minimum-wage-increase-inflation.asp

22. economist.com/graphic-detail/2021/02/02/global-democracy-has-a — very-bad-year

23. Victimhood: The affective politics of vulnerability. Lille Chouliaraki

24. theguardian.com/commentisfree/cifamerica/ 2010/nov/06/ben-bernanke-qe2-quantitave-easing

CHAPTER 3

1. twitter.com/robinbrooksiif/status/1339270749366972416

2. 'How the pandemic is forcing managers to work harder' The economist

3. Twitter.com/adam_tooze/status/1314287150184181760

CHAPTER 4

1. lrb.co.uk/the-paper/v42/n15/adam-tooze/whose-century

2. madeinchina.com/2019/11/12/chinese-communist-party-acess-to-private-enterprises/

3. carnegieedowment.org/chinafinancialmarkets/75355

4. reuters.com/article/china-bans-connect-idUSL5N2F304R

5. 'Is an infrastructure boomin the works' The economist

6. ft.com/content/facfe2cf-c78e-4085-882e-fdac59f1329d

7. 'Should th Fed cut rates below zero?' The economist

8. 'A shift from paper to virtual cash will empower central banks' The economist

9. en.wikipedia.org/wiki/modern_monetary_theory

10. dianeosis.org/2020/05/ena-vasiko-eisodima-gia-olous/

11. Good economics for hard times. Abhijit Banerjee, Esther Duflo

CHAPTER 5

1. Ανταποκρίσεις από τον 21º αιώνα. Romanos Gerodimos
2. en.wikipedia.org/wiki/bretton-woods-system
3. thebalance.com/world-currency-3305931
4. bis.org/pupl/bisbull32.pdf
5. The case for people's quantitative easing. France Coppola
6. ft.com/content/fcb05366-a3fb-4946-a026-5188d841b4a5

CHAPTER 6

1. statista.com/statistics/236943/global-advertising-spending/

2. https://noahpinion.substack.com/p/the-return-of-the-macro-wars

3. More from less. Andrew McAfee

4. Good economics for hard times. Abhijit Banerjee, Esther Duflo

5. Economist.com/finance-and-economics/2021/04/08/house-prices-in-the-rich-world-are-booming

CHAPTER 7

1. en.wikipedia.org/wiki/pensions_crisis

2. data.oecd.org/socialexp/pension-spending.htm

3. bloomberg.com/news/articles/2019-11-14/severe-15-8-trillion-pension-crisis-looms-worldwide-g-30-says

4. economist.com/leaders/2021/03/06/how-to-make-a-social-safety-net-for-the-post-covid-world

CHAPTER 8

1. Bullshit jobs. David Graeber
2. 'Workism is making American miserable' Derek Thompson. The atlantic
3. Good economics for hard times. Abhijit Banerjee, Esther Duflo